Miss Lloyd remembers ...

AN AUTOBIOGRAPHY

Noreen Lloyd

Miss Lloyd remembers ...
Published on behalf of the author
in Wales in 2007 by
BRIDGE BOOKS
61 PARK AVENUE
WREXHAM
LL12 7AW

CIP Data for this book is available
from the British Library

ISBN 978-1-84494-037-0

Printed and bound by
Cromwell Press Ltd
Trowbridge

This book is dedicated to

OLIVER

who cannot read or understand it,
but is my closest companion and friend.

Acknowledgements

My sincere thanks to my two nieces, my nephew and their families, for their help and support over the years and for their help in focusing certain blurred memories for this book. My thanks also to the scribe, Valerie Bond, who both wrote and illustrated and her friend Jean who edited and refined the text.

Introducing the scribe

Although my motivation in suggesting to Miss Lloyd that we write this book was mainly to forge a link between client and carer, as the work grew I felt it could be of interest to others, even if I only managed to capture a way of life that has not so much changed, but one that has gone into hiding. Miss Lloyd was born into a family of landed, but not titled, gentry. A family that has been landowners for generations and by careful management, tight fiscal policies and well-chosen marriages has held on to its inheritance. I was born middle class with no inheritance, but with the conviction that the world was my oyster and nothing I really wanted to do was impossible. Fortunately, I never wanted to climb Everest. As a youngster, I showed remarkably little curiosity about the past and my regrets in not asking the right questions when I had the opportunity have possibly influenced my attempts to ask the right questions of Miss Lloyd.

My grandfather was born in Tasmania. During my student years, I would often stay with my grandparents in Berkshire to enjoy a weekend away from London. We always talked of the present, never the past, and so I never asked my grandfather, 'Why did great grandfather go to Tasmania? How long did you live there? Why did your father decide to bring his family back?' I never asked about their early struggles in London, or even about the death of my grandmother and his second marriage to the remarkable lady who was the grandmother I knew. She too lived to receive a telegram from the Queen, but the last time I saw her she was in her nineties and very deaf. My voice could not penetrate the wall of silence. The time to ask questions of the past had gone.

My father had an interesting and adventurous life. In his sixties, ill-health forced inactivity and he tried to write a book. After a while, he gave up saying that he could not avoid an excessive use of the personal pronoun. If only one of us had said please forget a literary masterpiece, just write for us so we learn a little of all you did and can tell your grandchildren.

Tales to tell that will remain untold. Historians and archaeologists continually search for clues to past lives. The Samuel Pepys and Anne Frank diaries have been avidly read. Early film footage of everyday life is compelling viewing.

I do not have any particular desire to record my own life, nor have I ever managed to keep a diary for longer than one week. I have been to interesting places but the decision to travel was usually made for me by my parents or my husband. I tended to go where the wind blew me rather than make a conscious effort to venture forth, and left alone with enough money would happily vegetate in one comfortable spot. I have never been particularly interested in history, and brushing away dirt with a small paintbrush off some artefact in a trench interests me even less. But I do like people and that is a prerequisite of my present occupation as a live-in carer. Frankly, I was surprised at how much enthusiasm the idea of becoming an author aroused in Miss Lloyd. She would lean forward in her chair, bright-eyed and with a slight smile, 'Get yourself a drink – now, where did we get to?'

The following is Miss Lloyd's story. Some of it is exactly as she dictated, other portions are my interpretation from her description, but every word has been read back to her for her approval. However, I did interrupt every now and then if I felt I could enlarge on the story or increase understanding. Miss Lloyd is now in her 104th year and may not be able to read this book, but to hold it in her hand and know it is her story will please her immensely.

Val Bond

CHAPTER ONE

It was October 1903 …

I was born a twin. My sister and I were identical, but she arrived first. We were living in Plymouth, as my father was in the Royal Navy and on the day of our birth, his ship signalled to shore, 'Congratulations on the event.'

My father replied, 'You mean the double event!' This reaction makes me think that maybe my arrival was unexpected.

My sister was half-a-pound heavier than I was. She was seven-and-a-half pounds, I was seven pounds – have some pity for our poor mother! The year was 1903 and the month was October. King Edward VII and Queen Alexandra were on the throne. My father was obliged to live on board ship but had rented a house on The Hoe for his family; this was 7, Windsor Terrace. A nanny was engaged to help mother look after us. When the weather was fine, Nanny would push us both in a pram along Plymouth Hoe; not that I can remember that far back.

We were named Mabel Iris Elfrida and Noreen Mary. Mabel was our mother's name, so to avoid confusion my sister was always called Iris and for no good reason, other than it was a shorter name, my parents always called me Mary. When I grew older, Mary was discarded and I became Noreen. Even later, nieces and nephews contracted Auntie Noreen, and family members now call me Arnie. Back in 1903, however, Mabel Iris Elfrida and Noreen Mary were christened in a church in Plymouth. My mother's brother, Leslie Falkiner became godfather to Iris; my father's brother Arthur was my godfather. The little church where the ceremony took place was bombed-out during the war and never rebuilt; instead, there is a small garden there.

My father's name was Pennant Athelwold Iremonger Lloyd. He was a captain in the Royal Navy. When he was sent to different base ports, we as a family followed him. Leaving Plymouth, we moved to Kinsale in Ireland and then on to Edinburgh, before my father decided he had had enough and left the service. Later, I learned that my mother was rather disappointed with this decision as she was hoping one day to be married to an admiral. My father may also have retired, as he was needed at Pentrehobyn, the family estate near Mold, Flintshire. My grandfather had died, and my father was his eldest son, so we moved inland to the family home in North Wales.

My earliest memories are of being in Kinsale when our nursery governess joined us and became very much a part of our lives for the next ten years. The memories are of being with her, more than living in

My mother – Mabel Rose

Ireland and I will tell you more about her later. My childhood home and the place that even today is the quintessence of the word 'home' to me, is the beautiful old house of Pentrehobyn.

My mother met my father when she was staying with friends in Tunbridge Wells. They were married in London and, as both her parents had died, her brother Leslie gave the bride away. She was quite a bit shorter than my father who was well over six-feet tall; she had brown hair and hazel eyes, and was considered quite a beauty as had her mother. Before she was married, my mother had her portrait painted and it was hung at the Royal Academy in London before joining other family portraits on the walls of Pentrehobyn. Iris and I inherited her height and build, but in looks, we were far more like my father. The Lloyds have rather prominent noses, high fore-heads and fine, often rather sparse hair. We were no beauties, but at least looked intelligent!

My father – Pennant Athelwold Iremonger Lloyd

My parents were both more than thirty-years-old when they met and married, so were no doubt pleased when we arrived the year after their wedding. However, we were to have no other brothers or sisters. I believe that my mother would have liked a larger family and I would have thought my father would have liked a son, but it was not to be.

My mother was well travelled and as a child had lived in France for a while, so spoke very good French. Her parents were both the children of baronets. I was told her mother, my grandmother, climbed Mont Blanc: she was not the first woman to do so, but I believe she was certainly one of the first.* Grandmother must have been quite a spirited lady and I wish I had met her. Her daughter was more reserved though she did enjoy living in London, going to the theatre and shopping, but after marrying my father, adapted well to country life. She was clever with a needle and made clothes for us when we were children.

---

* Miss Lloyd's nephew has a framed certificate to confirm that 6 August 1876, Madame Falkiner climbed to the summit of Mont Blanc.

My father, having been a senior naval officer, enjoyed social gatherings and having friends round for dinner, and my mother was a good hostess, making people feel welcome. She was a quiet, calm person, well-organised and capable, and an ideal partner for my father who was more outgoing. I do not ever remember them arguing; if they did it was never while we were around. My father tended to run the house as he had run a ship, and at times my mother found that a bit tiresome. He would issue his orders to the staff but mother, with typical feminine guile, would still manage to get things done her way, determined that when it came to running a house, she should have the final say. If my father was aware that his orders were being countermanded nothing was said, and his good sense of humour probably defused any marital conflict. He was kept busy with the management of the Pentrehobyn estate for, although he employed an agent in Mold, there was still a lot that required his personal attention.

Interruption ...

At the top of the stairs in the house where Miss Lloyd now lives, there is a framed photograph of Captain Pennant Athelwold Lloyd hanging on the wall by the window. He is in uniform, standing with one hand behind his back. An upright figure, he could almost be described as imperious except for a twist to his mouth that discloses a quirk of humour. This man you feel would command other men fairly and firmly, but back in the wardroom would pour a gin and tonic and tell a good story, even one against himself. The photograph has had the background bleached away and has been delicately retouched; a warmth of colour on his face, a flash of blue on his uniform, with yellow on the brass buttons and on the braiding on his sleeves and cap. On the wall on the other side of the window hangs a framed, similarly retouched photograph of his daughter in the uniform of a WRNS Second Officer taken during the Second World War. The family likeness is unmistakeable, though Miss Noreen Lloyd is slightly more relaxed and has a big, friendly smile.

With us, my father was an affectionate man and would often give us both a hug and a kiss. From the time we first stood up, Iris and I did everything together. Our friends used to refer to us simply as 'the Twins.' I have been asked to describe my sister, but I cannot other than to say she was just like me, but nicer! A relation of ours once said that as children, if we were asked a question, we would turn to look at each other and pause as if mentally exchanging thoughts, before one of us would reply.

Mother and her twins, 1904

Having said that Iris was like me but nicer, perhaps I had better try to describe myself. In looks, as I mentioned earlier, I was a typical Lloyd; high forehead, fine brown hair, brown eyes, a long face and strong teeth. I can flash a smile to knock you out, even today! I can be impatient, and like to get my own way. I think I am kind and should anyone need my help, I would do my best to do what I could. Most of the time as children we only had each other for company but on the odd occasion, when thrust into the company of other children, we mixed in easily enough. We were perhaps reserved, but not shy. Good manners were insisted upon, and politeness dictated a concern for the feelings of others. Does that sound boring? I think I had a streak of adventure in me more so than Iris. I would be the first one to explore a new path or climb up a tree, Iris would follow. We were both very active children not the sort to sit with a good book or do needlework. I have noticed the same trait in both my nieces; they move quickly and can make an instant decision and act upon it.

My father only enjoyed a few years away from the Navy. In 1914, the First World War began and he was called up to serve as Senior Naval

Officer in Folkestone, Kent. Once more, we all moved home to be near him. Mother, Iris and I, together with our nursery governess, stayed in a boarding house on the sea front and my father, as before, slept on board his ship. He was invalided out before the end of the war – it was the start of the cancer – and we returned to Pentrehobyn. When he became very ill, a bed was made up in the drawing room and a nurse brought in to help look after him. The cancer must have spread to his liver, for I remember being quite horrified when visiting him for what was in fact the last time, to see that his skin was so yellow.

My mother was married for just fourteen years before becoming a widow. She never married again, which did not surprise me. She said that had she not met my father, she probably would not have married at all. I am sure it was not for lack of suitors that she felt that way. My sister and I were quite happy with her decision, as we did not like the idea of anyone replacing our father.

CHAPTER TWO

The old house – Pentrehobyn

Other than the sadness caused by my father's ill-health and subsequent death, my sister and I had a wonderful childhood. We grew up in such lovely surroundings and enjoyed the freedom of country living. The house we lived in was built by my ancestor, Edward Lloyd, on the site of an even earlier building built in 1540 and that date can be seen over the front door. The house overlooks splendid lawns where we used to play tennis. A good-sized kitchen garden supplied vegetables for the house and the usual favourite soft fruits such as gooseberries and blackcurrants. There was no orchard as such, but there were several fruit trees and in the autumn, we would pick apples, pears and plums. At the entrance to Pentrehobyn is a lodge where the gardener lived when I was a child. From the lodge, the drive leads straight to the main house that is set back and hidden from the road by a hedge. Amongst the outbuildings surrounding the house, is stabling that could have accommodated several horses, but we only ever had the one pony called Poppy. Large trees grow in the parkland around the house; oak, elm and ash, with a fine row of lime trees planted behind the house. The fields that are also part of the property were let for grazing, usually for sheep, and still are today.

We had a peacock and a peahen that had the freedom of the grounds. They went by the names of Caesar and Cleopatra. Cleopatra, incidentally, was also the name of my father's ship. Peacocks tend to be noisy birds but are beautiful to have around. The gardener was none too fond of them as they would eat his plants and make hollows in the flowerbeds as though nesting. Eventually they were sent to a zoo, or so I was told.

Close to the house, Edward Lloyd had built accommodation for the use of poor wayfarers travelling through the area. Known as *Lletau* (Welsh for a place to stay), they are a row of eight cell-like rooms. Each room has a low wooden entrance-door and, on opening the door, a small windowless vaulted chamber is revealed, seven-feet wide by five-feet deep. The wayfarers must have been short in stature as the highest part of the room is barely six feet. These little cell-like rooms are not completely airless as, on either side of the door, there are keyhole-shaped openings small enough to let in air, but not an intruder larger than a mouse. Presumably a couple of forkfuls of straw would be tossed in to provide a bed. There are no records that I know of to indicate if these travellers had to pay to stay in these rooms.

At the end of these rooms is a double-storey building that at one time

Lletau at Pentrehobyn

accommodated the overseer. Food was given to the travellers, and I was told that a wooden post had spoons and forks tied to it for their use. Even in those early days, guests were likely to walk off with the cutlery it seems. Nowadays the *lletau* are used as storage rooms. I think that modern travellers or tourists would expect more than the offer of these primitive rooms. They are of historical interest though and I am told that there is only one other house where *lletau* were built, but I do not know the location of this house.The plaque on the wall outside reads:

THESE LLETTAI WERE ERECTED BY MR. E. LLOYD WHEN HE BUILT PENTREHOBYN. AFTER THE SUPPRESSION OF THE MONASTRIES BY HENRY VIII THERE WERE NO RESTING PLACES FOR THE POOR MOVING FROM ONE PLACE TO ANOTHER. THE BENEVOLENCE OF MR. E. LLOYD SUPPLIED THIS MUCH NEEDED WANT.

The house of Pentrehobyn is built in the shape of an 'H'. It has a slate-tiled roof with gables on both legs of the 'H', mullioned windows and tall chimneys. Some people find the house a bit forbidding, but it is home to me and the memories of my childhood there are good. As it is still owned by family, I am able to revisit the past there. The house has been changed and added to since it was originally built and comfort items such as central-heating put in, and a lift to make it easier for an elderly person to reach the bedrooms on the first floor. The second floor was at one time servants' quarters; small rooms built between the large oak beams supporting the roof. Now it has all been opened up and a bathroom has been added for the bedrooms there. The main bedrooms on the first floor have been modernised and another bathroom added where the schoolroom used to be. So now each of the four bedrooms on that floor has its own bathroom. When I was a child, there was only one bathroom on the first floor and the servants had to carry water up to the top floor for their ablutions.

When you go through the main door into Pentrehobyn, you first come into a hall and at the end of this hall is the main staircase. An unusual carved wooden post has been incorporated into the banisters at

18

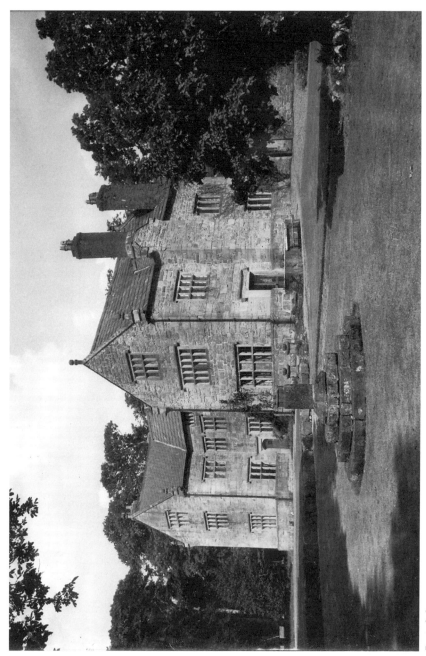

Pentrehobyn

the bottom of this staircase. According to Christopher Hussey, the author of a magazine article written about the house, it is an *ysbûr*, dating back to medieval times and is likely to have been part of a buffet. It was brought across from the old farmhouse at Glan Hafon that is part of the Llangynog estate in the Tanat valley also owned by Lloyd family members. The carving on this post is remarkable being both bold and decorative.

Main staircase with the ysbûr on the right

If, from this entrance hall, you turn through a door immediately to the right, you will come into the main hall and turning to the left would take you into the dining room. The main hall is oak panelled and family portraits hang on the walls. There is a large open fireplace with a decorative carved oak over-mantel with the arms of Lloyd of Pentrehobyn and the arms of Morgan of Gwylgre, the family of Edward Lloyd's wife, Margaret. Nowadays when the fire is lit, the family in residence, my nephew, will entertain friends in this room as a large sofa and chairs are round the fire. When I was a child, the sofa and chairs were not round the fire, the main hall had a big table in the middle that has since been moved into the dining room, and the study was the place to sit and relax, or if entertaining guests, the drawing room would be used. Originally, and this was even before my time, the main staircase came down into this hall. The main staircase is oak and perhaps should be referred to as the 'moving staircase.' As it tended to make the main hall draughty, it was moved to come down into the entrance hall near the front door. In later years when Iris, my twin sister was running the house, it was moved again, this time further back and away from the front door to where it is today.

The dining room too has another highly decorative carved oak over-mantel. The date carved on it is 1546 with the initials 'E Ll' and 'M Ll' (Lloyd). Experts believe that this date is not the date of the panel although the Royal Arms, with the Welsh dragon, are those of the Tudor monarchs. It was a common, but misleading, practice in Wales at that time to commemorate forbears.

The over-mantel is believed to be early seventeenth century. There are four female figures depicted in early Elizabethan costume with the small ruffs. I have been told that they represent the cardinal virtues of temperance, prudence, justice and fortitude. These four are positioned to frame the Royal Arms in the middle and two other shields on either side. The shields in the side panels depict the arms attributed to Edwin ap Goronwy, Prince of Tegeingl, also known as Edwin of Rhual, who lived in the eleventh century. Along the top of this over mantel there is a charming frieze depicting animals of the fables; dogs, a stag, a rabbit, a bear and a goose confronting a fox.

A bird appears on the Lloyd crest and is used elsewhere as decoration. The bird is the Cornish chough. Quite how a Cornish bird flew onto Welsh arms I can only guess. It appears decoratively carved in marble on either side of the fireplace in the drawing room as well as in the four quarters round a cross on the arms and on the top.

On one wall, there is a fine portrait of Pennant Athelwold Lloyd, my paternal grandfather. He was the only grandparent Iris and I knew and he died when we were six years old. My mother's parents both died before she married.

The table in the dining room can seat ten people. As children, my sister and I would join our parents at this table for luncheon: This was the main meal of the day. Breakfast and supper we would have in the nursery upstairs. When the dining room was in use in winter, the fire would be lit; the larger fireplace in the main hall would have a big log fire blazing in the hearth all day to help heat the surrounding rooms. The house is now more efficiently centrally heated but I do not remember ever feeling the cold when living there as a child.

I will always love Pentrehobyn and have several photographs of it; these are rather formal portraits that do not match the pictures etched in my memory.

CHAPTER THREE

Alice Jones is no good

When I was a child, there were servants in the house. There was a cook, a parlour maid, a housemaid, and a between-maid, commonly known as a 'tweeny.' The tweeny was usually a young girl straight from school and working in the house would be her first job. She would be immediately answerable to the cook and spent a lot of her time preparing vegetables. All the servants lived on the premises, their rooms being up on the top floor, and downstairs there was a sitting room adjacent to the kitchen set aside for their use. As children, Iris and I would slip down into this room to enjoy their company. They used to teach us songs and chat to us about their families.

> Alice Jones is no good,
> Chop her up for firewood,
> When she's dead,
> Cut her head,
> And make her into currant bread.

Isn't it strange that after more than ninety-five years that silly rhyme still sticks in my head?

My mother was a little concerned that, in seeking the company of the servants, we might hear things that she would consider unsuitable for young people, but she never forbade us to speak or be with them.

The staff all wore uniforms. Their everyday wear would be striped cotton but for waiting at table, the servants on duty would change into a smarter uniform consisting of a dark-red dress, protected with white apron, and with a small white cap on their heads. The staff then was all female, but in my grandfather's day, there had been a butler employed. The food store next to the kitchen was always kept locked and each day after discussing the menu with my mother, the cook would come to the storeroom with empty jars where my mother would hand out the dry-goods necessary for the day's meals. We had several different cooks while I was a child, but no names stand out in my memory. I suppose all were referred to simply as 'Cook'. As my father enjoyed inviting guests for dinner, the cook was kept quite busy. I remember that all the cooks were good at making puddings. I had a sweet tooth and particularly enjoyed the pudding that was called 'chocolate shape', a blancmange of sorts. There were no handy supermarkets with instant puddings in those days, so the cooks had to have a good assortment of recipes for everyday and special occasions and for a variety of cakes and biscuits for tea. All cooking was done on a kitchen range and as it was a time before refrigerators, a large, cold, slate-lined, walk-in larder kept food cool. There were no washing machines or tumble dryers either and yet it was a time when servants wore crisp white starched aprons and small children wore white cotton dresses. Table linen was white damask and everyone used a napkin. Floors would be polished by a maid on her knees. Brushes and dustpans were used in place of vacuum cleaners. People today feel that perhaps we were spoilt by having servants but Pentrehobyn is a large house, and without the modern appliances, it would have been impossible for one person to manage and quite impossible to entertain guests in the style expected.

One day a year was Rent Day when the tenants of the estate came to pay their rent. My mother entertained them in the hall while they waited to go into the study one at a time. After all the rents had been paid, the tenants were invited to luncheon. The menu never varied and was always roast beef and boiled mutton followed by apple tart and plum pudding, washed down no doubt with beer. My sister and I used

Aunt Elfrida

to join them for the luncheon. The estate had four farms and a few cottages that were let separately. Strangely, I can only remember my uncle hosting this event, though my father must have done it before him – but we were probably too young to participate.

The drawing room leads off the main hall: it was, and still is, a pleasant, large room with comfortable armchairs and a sofa. Most of the furniture is antique, handed down through the family. As children, we rarely went into this room, unless some visitor wished to meet us. A French door led into a conservatory, with a further door leading out to the garden. Eventually, when the timbers rotted and it became unsafe, the conservatory was demolished. It is surprising how much lighter the drawing room seems now the conservatory has gone.

On the walls in the drawing room are family portraits including two large paintings of my aunts: these are my father's sisters, Mary and Elfrida. When these two young Victorian ladies married, they became Mrs Iremonger and Mrs Campbell. Both are portrayed seated and Aunt Elfrida is holding a little cat. My parents had their portraits painted and when we were children, the two portraits hung together in the study. Neither my sister nor I had our portraits painted and, so far, none of the younger generation has either; we will fade away with no young children gazing up at our portraits. We never wondered at our ancestors, but just accepted them as one would wallpaper. There are other portraits of various members of the Lloyd family all around the house and having lived with them for so many years, it seems strange that in fact I know very little or nothing about them. One I know is of a Mary Lloyd, but to whom she was married and when, I am not sure.

Interruption ...

There are family names that recur through the generations – Edward of course, Athelwold, Mary, Elfrida and Pennant. There are several Lloyds in Llangynog, and to avoid confusion, Miss Lloyd is often referred to as Miss Pennant Lloyd after her father. Pennant is a name that crops up quite a lot in Wales. Translated it means head of the river or valley. Pennant is also used as a girl's name.

Miss Lloyd is surprisingly vague when asked about family history. It is obviously of little interest to her, having always been more concerned with life as it was going on around her then and as it is now. There are a lot of questions regarding the Lloyd's past history that I am sure would reward anyone prepared to spend the time searching back through parish records and census lists. I personally have not the time, nor the inclination, to follow the threads myself, but would be interested to learn more of Edward Lloyd. From where did the wealth come that built the great house? Did the family own the house that was there before Pentrehobyn was built? Estates grow when marriage brings properties together, and that might explain the distance between the Pentrehobyn and Llangynog estates. But who and when? Research into family history has only recently become a popular pastime. The Lloyds did not keep diaries, so the information in this book has been drawn from Miss Lloyd's remarkable memory and that is selective, but still sufficient I trust, to paint a picture of her life and times.

My father had three brothers and two sisters. His two elder brothers died before him, one as a child, and the other as a young man at sea. His brother Arthur, the youngest of the family, and who never married, was a wonderful person, and like a father to us after our father died. He had served in the army during the Boer War and been awarded the DSO. When Uncle Arthur sold the cottage he had in Suffolk, he moved to the Llangynog estate in the Tanat valley on the way to Bala, and lived in the

Uncle Arthur

house where I live now. He did this to be nearer to us, as Llangynog is only about fifty miles from Pentrehobyn, and he was able to travel over to see us at least once a month. My grandfather used to write poetry and he wrote a poem about Arthur. I do not have a copy of it but remember one line, 'He will be loved until the end, my Arthur.' And he was!

The house near Mold was always the centre for the family. Although we were direct descendants of Edward Lloyd who built the house, our name should have been Iremonger, but it was changed to Lloyd; first by my great uncle who inherited Pentrehobyn from his grandmother, Margaret Thomas, and then by my grandfather, Pennant Athelwold Iremonger. The name change was a condition of the inheritance. Aunt Mary married a cousin and went back from Lloyd to Iremonger. My sister and I were the only Lloyd children of the next generation. There are no more sons to carry the name forward and the name Lloyd will once more leave Pentrehobyn.

Interruption ...

On a table upstairs in Miss Lloyd's house is the massive tome that is Burke's Landed Gentry. *I looked up Lloyd, but the Lloyds mentioned did not appear to have any link with the Lloyd of Pentre Hobyn. Iremonger did yield further information. William Iremonger (1776–1852) married Pennant, the youngest daughter of Rice Thomas of Coed Helen, Carnarfonshire. She bore him five sons, William, Thomas, Frederick Pennant and Henry. The third son, Frederick Assheton Lloyd, assumed the surname Lloyd in 1872 in compliance with the testamentary injunction of his grandmother, Margaret Thomas. Frederick married twice but had no issue. The fourth son, Pennant Athelwold Lloyd, D.L., J.P., of Pentre Hobyn, High Sheriff of Flintshire, assumed the surname Lloyd in 1872 for the same reason as his brother. He married Mary, daughter of Pryce Jones of Cyfronydd, Montgomeryshire and they had issue: Pennant Athelwold Iremonger Lloyd, (father of the twins, and their details are listed there); the two girls Mary and Elfrida; and finally Arthur. Two things intrigue me here: why did two brothers change their surname to Lloyd in the same year? and, although Miss Lloyd was positive that her father had two older brothers, there is no mention of them in* Burke's. *These anomalies would make a historian's nose twitch and no doubt the information is out there somewhere in another dusty tome.*

The house is old. Old buildings are often known to have ghosts and Pentrehobyn is no exception. One visitor to the house claimed to have seen a little old man leaving one of the upstairs bedrooms and her pet dog would not enter that room.

About ten years ago, when staying at the house, I slept downstairs in the study as there was a power cut and the lift up to the bedrooms could not be used. Being more than ninety-years-old, arthritis was beginning to trouble me. Comfortably settled on the sofa with pillows and blankets, I suddenly noticed the door opening and a figure going across to the chest that opens to reveal a hidden staircase leading to a small cellar. Presuming it was someone requiring a late nightcap, as wine, etc, was kept in that cellar, I decided to speak to my nephew about it in the morning. Then the figure reappeared this time standing by the fireplace. Thinking I had better say something, I asked, 'Are you frightened by the fire?' The figure half turned towards me and I saw to my surprise that it was my twin sister who had died in 1992. She did not look directly at me and made no gesture, nor did she speak, but simply faded away. Although not scared by the vision, and maybe it was just a very vivid dream, I would never again sleep in the study.

Captain Lloyd with the twins

The house was marvellous for family occasions and hosted many birthday parties and family gatherings at Christmas. When we were about eighteen-years-old, my sister and I had a 'coming out' dance in the main hall. It was an evening affair. We had a band for dancing and a buffet supper. It was I think, our first formal occasion and the first time we dressed for an evening event. We danced a lot and it was tremendous fun. Having five bedrooms, plus what had been servants' quarters in the attics, we could easily accommodate guests, so cousins and friends were able to stay the night if they had travelled from a distance. When my sister Iris was married at the church in Mold, her reception was at the house and most recent of all, I was taken back to the house for a family party to celebrate my hundredth birthday.

When we were children, my sister and I had a nanny and later a nursery governess. The nursery governess, Quint, first became part of the family when we were living in Kinsale and we were devoted to her. This young Irish girl came with us to Mold and was with us when my father became ill and being nursed at home. Having her there made life a little easier for my mother. Knowing we were in safe hands, enabled her to concentrate on my father's needs. On the day my father died, Quint was the one who broke the news to us and then took us through to our mother. We shared a bed that night, mother, Iris and I, to comfort each other, as if with touch and warmth we could ease the grief.

CHAPTER FOUR

A little learning

Earlier, I promised to tell you a little more about our nursery governess, Quint. Her name was Elizabeth Quint but we had our own name for her and called her Dezel. This was a name we had made up and she was quite happy to be called by it. Typically Irish in that she had dark hair and blue eyes, she talked as if she had kissed the stone at Blarney Castle. She was medium to tall in height and quick moving, and could always find something for us to do on a dull, rainy, winter's evening. She was not afraid of anything or anyone, and my mother found that when she asked us a question, it was often Dezel who answered for us. Dezel must have been with us for more than ten years and our first efforts at reading and writing would have been under her instruction. Once a year, she would return home to Kinsale for a holiday and one day told us she had met a young man who had asked her to marry him. Proudly she showed us the ring on her finger. Iris and I must have been in our early teens then and our mother decided we needed a more experienced governess. And so Dezel left us and, with her young man, sailed off to Canada and married him there. Whenever they came back for a visit, they always came to see us and so we kept in touch. She never had a family of her own, and that was sad as she had a natural way with children, enjoying them as much as they enjoyed her. Dezel and her husband eventually returned to Britain and lived in Norfolk. She died in 1963, the same year as my mother.

As a child, my mother had been sent away to boarding school in

Tunbridge Wells. It was reputably a very good school but she was extremely unhappy there and did not wish her twins to have a similar experience. Therefore, it was decided that we would be educated at home. I am not sure that it was the right decision as although there may be some advantages in having one-to-one teaching, a lot rests on the knowledge, patience and skill of the person teaching. Most children benefit more from the competition with their peers, plus the variety of more than one teacher.

The twins with Pharoah

Our schoolroom was upstairs, conveniently on the same floor as our bedrooms. Three different governesses taught us over the years; Miss Long, Miss Berry and Miss Hill. They taught us reading, writing and arithmetic, history, geography and some French.

Miss Long, unlike her name, did not stay long. She, poor soul, did not enjoy good health and so returned home. Miss Berry we liked a lot. She was exceptionally knowledgeable and a good teacher, but perhaps two little girls were one too many and after a year or so she left. She kept in touch and sent us postcards. Later she married and became Lady Outram. The last governess, Miss Hill, stayed on until the end. She was older than the other two and used to dye her hair to hide the grey. We did not like her and lessons became tedious.

As my mother spoke such good French, and was keen that we also acquired a good accent, extra lessons were arranged. Our teacher was French and neither of us liked her very much. Music was another extra lesson arranged by my mother and we did not like our music teacher either. All young ladies were expected to play the piano, but we hated it.

No one in our family was musical, even with such a Welsh name as Lloyd!

Although piano lessons were not favoured, we did enjoy dancing and one afternoon a week, went to Chester by train for dancing classes. Miss Hammond was in charge, assisted by Miss Price. We learnt the waltz, the quickstep and the foxtrot, but none of the more flamboyant Latin-American dances that had yet to become popular. It was an opportunity for us to meet other girls of our own age and as far as we were concerned, dancing was the highlight of our week. There were no boys at these classes. Our governess used to accompany us and often our mother came too, as it gave her a chance to shop in Chester.

I do not think either of us was particularly good at our lessons. There was no way of judging, even though our governess would set us tests and examinations, as we were not in competition with other children. Our governess lived in the house during term time, when the schools had their holidays so did we, and the governess went home for her holiday.

One Christmas, there was a fancy dress dance in the Town Hall in Mold, the proceeds of which were earmarked for some charity or other. Iris and I went as Quaker girls and wore grey dresses with white collars, white aprons and bonnets on our heads. Our sombre dresses must have stood out against the bright colours of some of the other costumes. Our cousins from Lincolnshire were visiting us at that time and joined in the fun. They were dressed as a policeman, a forget-me-not and the Knave of Hearts. The youngest cousin, a toddler then, was dressed as Cupid. He looked charming with his round and rosy cheeks. His costume had small wings attached to the back of the bodice and he had a bow and arrow slung around his waist. He was protesting loudly for all to hear, 'I don't want to go as Stupid'!

Even as a child, I was fond of animals. The first dog I can remember was a black and white wire-haired terrier called Pharaoh, who was with us when we lived in Kinsale. He used to go and eat the blackberries off the bushes in the garden, a habit that we found amusing and unusual for a dog. Pharaoh came with us when we moved to Edinburgh and eventually on to the house near Mold. When we got to Pentrehobyn, there was already a dog there, a collie called Mike. Fortunately, both dogs liked each other and both lived to a good old age and are buried there. At one time, there were three dogs at Pentrehobyn. My mother had a spaniel called Joy, my sister had an Airedale and I had another wire-haired terrier. I also had a cat called Punch and my sister of course had the cat called Judy. There was also a pony which was rarely ridden, mostly harnessed to a trap to drive us to the local village. We were entirely responsible for our animals and had to feed and groom them ourselves. We took the dogs with us when we went walking. My favourite destination was a nearby farm where I used to beg to see the animals. We bought a few pullets from this farmer with our pocket money and kept them in an enclosure until eventually they were big enough to lay eggs for the house. This, I suppose, might be considered my first little attempt at farming.

CHAPTER FIVE

Coming Out

Being identical twins, we were dressed alike as children. This never concerned us particularly. We had no strong desire to prove our individuality, nor did we play twin tricks. I do not say we never quarrelled, but on the whole, we were happy doing things together. When it came to birthdays and Christmas though, even if our dresses were identical, we had different gifts, usually hinted at to my mother beforehand. Our friends knew us well enough to know who was who, but I do not believe our family doctor ever sorted us out. As we grew older, our different interests developed and became more apparent and we began to dress differently. I was very much an outdoor person whereas Iris preferred indoor activities.

During the First World War, the local people of Mold decided to put on variety concerts to raise money to help with the war effort. With encouraging words from my mother, such as, 'Your Country Needs You', we were sent off to do recitations. We did not go on stage together. Iris would be called upon first, and then I would follow after other performers had done their bit. We recited two poems each. I remember one that Iris did was 'The Old Clock on the Stairs', and I recited the popular poems, 'If', by Rudyard Kipling and 'Be Thorough Boys!' All very uplifting. The other performers were also local people, singing or playing an instrument. We were the youngest and probably the most reluctant of all.

After my father died, it must have been difficult for my mother to continue running the large house. She was a gentle lady who enjoyed her garden, but also dutifully became involved in the local community via the church and the Cottage Hospital. To raise money for the Cottage Hospital, my mother once took over the local cinema and persuaded three friends from Kent to come and put on a play. I can remember the names of two of them, the sisters Hawthorne and Philippa Barnes. The third player was a friend of theirs who was related to a well-known member of the Liberal party, but her name escapes me. All three stayed with us at Pentrehobyn.

Mother — dressed for the Palace

The play, or plays, as I believe there was more than one, were only on for three days, and Iris and I were asked to sell programmes. We were also allowed to stand at the back and watch the performance. We thought they were very good and so did the audience judging by the applause. The plays were a great success and raised a lot of money. Although not one to go on stage herself, my mother was good at persuading others, particularly if it was for a good cause.

I have a framed photograph of my mother looking very elegant in the dress she wore on the day we were presented at Court. That was another milestone in our lives when the chrysalis of childhood cracked open and two young ladies emerged bright eyed and curious. My sister and I were about twenty-years-old when my mother sent our names forward and we were duly notified of the day when we would be presented to King George and Queen Mary. Our cousin, Naomi Falkiner was to be presented at the same time. She was the forget-me-not at the fancy dress dance when we were teenagers; this time, however, the dressmaker was called on to make completely different costumes. Elegant, fashionable, full-length dresses were required now. These dresses had trains of lace that hung from the shoulders and swept the floor behind us. As was the fashion, we wore long white kid-gloves and a band of ribbon came across our foreheads and to the back of our heads, where headdresses of feathers were attached to a veil. The veils fell down to our waists and the dresses came down to our ankles. Elegant court shoes completed our ensembles.

We stayed in a hotel in London, and on the day we were to be presented, a hired car came to collect us and we drove in procession down The Mall with all the other young ladies who were to be presented on that day. It was springtime, and the weather was still quite fresh so we wore coats over our presentation gowns. Arriving at Buckingham Palace, we left our coats in a cloakroom before being ushered into an antechamber where we waited until our names were called. At last we heard, 'Mrs Pennant Lloyd presenting her two daughters, Miss Iris

Lloyd and Miss Noreen Lloyd'. Moving, we hoped, with grace and dignity, we went through the door and curtsied first to Queen Mary and then to King George V. Our curtsies were acknowledged by a slight dip of a royal head, but no words were spoken. Then we moved off into another room to have a stand-up tea. I vaguely remember a very good spread of small cakes, sandwiches and other delights, and tea served in delicate china cups.

After the presentation, we returned to our quiet life in Wales. Many of the

Presenting Miss Noreen Lloyd

girls presented that day went on to have a 'London Season' involving many social events and parties. Naomi, the 'forget-me-not', was one of them, and in fact had two seasons before she turned down a proposal of marriage and decided instead to become a nun. She joined the Order of the Holy Sepulchre and lived all her life in a convent in Chelmsford. She had been a pupil at a school run by nuns, and so it was an easy transition for her to join a convent. In later years, when convent rules tended to be less rigid, she came and stayed with me in my house in Llangynog for a couple of days. She seemed very happy and contented with her chosen life. Over the years, we had visited her quite often but this was the first time she had been permitted to visit me. To this day, I find it hard to understand her decision to become a nun. She was as a sister to us as she and her three brothers stayed with us so often during the holidays when we were young.

We were by no means country bumpkins, for my mother would take us up to London for a 'theatre week' every so often. None of us fancied the ballet or the opera, but we did enjoy musicals. We saw all the big musicals of the day, from *Bitter Sweet* to *My Fair Lady*, and the various Gilbert and Sullivan operettas, *The Mikado*, *The Pirates of Penzance*, to name just two, but our real preference was to see a good straight play. On our trips to London, we also gradually took in all the tourist attractions and visited Madame Tussauds, the Tower of London, St Paul's Cathedral and Westminster Abbey.

My mother belonged to a women's club, Sesame, in the West End, and the three of us would stay there when in London. Later, I belonged to the Naval and Military Club in Piccadilly, and that was where I stayed on visits to the capital city. Although I never wanted to live in London, I enjoyed my visits there. Wandering round the shops by day and then off to the theatre in the evening. All the members of our family enjoyed the theatre and far more recently I went to see *Cats* twice, once with my sister, and once with her daughter Mary. Maybe its animal connection particularly appealed to me, for I loved that show.

CHAPTER SIX

Holidays

Returning once more to our childhood years, and the joys of the summer holiday. All our family seem to enjoy world travel even when it was not as easy as it is today and Iris and I were taken several times to the Continent. The first holiday abroad that I can remember was when my father was still alive and we all went to Montreux in Switzerland. My parents had honeymooned there so were happy to revisit it with us. I do not remember much about it, but know we stayed in a flat and were able to watch people skiing past our building. A friend of my mother's came with us and both my sister and I remember being terrified when she picked us up in turn and dangled us over the balcony. We could not have been more than five or six years old and maybe she thought she was amusing us. Looking back it seems a strange thing to do and we certainly never forgot it. As far as I know neither my mother nor my father went skiing but they did come tobogganing with us. Come to think of it, tobogganing was the only outdoor sporting activity that I can remember my parents enjoying.

After my father died, my mother took us to Paris and then on to Rome. I suppose we did all the usual touristy things in Paris; the Eiffel Tower, the Champs Elysee and the Mona Lisa. Similarly in Rome, where I remember throwing coins into the Trevi Fountain to ensure my return one day – but I never did.

Other holidays were spent in Britain. We would go to the seaside not very far from Mold, to a village called Rhos-on-Sea near Colwyn Bay. We stayed in a small boarding house facing the sea and went back there several years. I never learned to swim, simply paddled. Iris did eventually learn to swim after she married and was living down in Cornwall. As children, we were content to collect shells, build sand-castles and ride donkeys on the beach. In other words, we did all the things that children love to do at the seaside.

While in my twenties, I went to stay for a few days with Aunt Elfrida in Perthshire, Scotland. Her house was a typical bleak Scottish house, a little on the cold side, though the welcome was warm enough. Uncle Jack was away in the army, but Aunt Elfrida's daughter Isabel, a little older than I, was there at that time. Isabel and I walked the hills amongst the heather together. Sometimes we saw deer or the shaggy highland cattle. We ate porridge and oatcakes; my taste for whisky came much later. Aunt Elfrida had two sons both of whom followed their father into the army. Their names were Colin and Archie. Colin was captured during the Second World War, escaped and eventually made his way back to Britain. Awarded the Military Cross, he went on to write a book about his adventures. Isabel was a very pretty girl; strangely, she never married, neither did Colin. Eventually, Isabel came to live in London and for many years worked there as a secretary to a doctor. Archie became a brigadier and was awarded the DSO and the OBE. After the war, he was appointed British Consul in Kobe, Japan. His second wife was Australian, and Australia is where he spent his last few years. The only one of the three to marry, Archie had a daughter, Mary Alice, who married a farmer in Perthshire. They have four children.

Some years later, Iris and I went back to France with our mother, this time to the southern part and a small town called Hyères in Var. Mother had been very ill with a lung infection and had spent some time in hospital. The doctors advised a complete rest and a holiday, so as soon as she was well enough the three of us set off. We travelled comfortably by train, apart from the ferry across the Channel of course. There was not a lot to do in Hyères, but that was how we wanted it and mother spent most of the time relaxing in the sun. Not wanting to leave her on her own for too long, Iris and I would sometimes make short excursions into the town to look at the shops. We stayed in Hyères for about a month. The warmer climate worked its magic and mother regained her strength.

Holiday over, it was time for further education. I went to an agricultural school in Kent to learn how to milk a cow and make butter and cheeses. The school was rather exclusive as it only took about six people at any one time. We lived on the premises, each of us having our own room. Both the instructors were women as were the pupils for co-education was rarely considered before the War. We had written work and hands-on practical farming. The animals kept there were cows and pigs but we had little to do with the pigs, concentrating more on the dairy side of farming. I can remember my first attempts at milking a cow. The cow in question was a gentle creature called 'Red Mansion'. I believe she was kept because of her patience when beginners such as me attempted to coax out the milk. As my hands are not very big I found milking difficult. I did, however, take to cheese making. The course lasted about six months and during that time, I watched a cow giving birth to a calf for the first time. Later when I had my own animals, I spent many an hour in a cowshed assisting with a difficult birth. At the end of the course, I felt quietly confident that I could look after cows and run a dairy and I looked forward to having a few animals of my own.

There was plenty of space at Pentrehobyn to have a small herd. There were outbuildings to use as milking sheds and a large outside larder with table-height slate slabs that converted easily into a dairy. I had to buy some equipment, such as a milk cooler and a trolley to move the heavy churns. As there was no running water, I had to carry this in by the bucket, but the cool room was pleasant both to work in and good for keeping my cheeses fresh until I took them to sell.

While I was learning farming, my sister went off to study domestic science for six months and became a very good cook. A skill never used

Pentrehobyn Dairy

to earn money but enjoyed by her husband and family.

Before beginning the serious business of earning a living, I did have one other holiday that I remember to this day as it was the first time I travelled alone. I thoroughly enjoyed the adventure. It was early in the 1920s and Aunt Elfrida's son, cousin Archie, who was stationed in Egypt, invited me to visit him. I travelled by ship and spent ten days with him and his wife in Cairo. Determined to sightsee as much as possible while there, I went off on my own one day and rode a camel to the pyramids. It was a very joggy ride not at all the swaying motion I expected from a 'ship of the desert.' In those days, women did not wear trousers and so suitably skirted I rode sidesaddle. The pyramids are quite a distance from Cairo and I was amazed by the stamina of the elderly man, who walked all the way there and all the way back again, leading my camel. Once there, I climbed to the top of a pyramid with the assistance of a guide. The view from the top was wonderful. You could see Cairo in the distance as well as other smaller pyramids, plus lots of sand. It is a pity, but necessary, that nowadays climbing up the pyramids is forbidden to preserve the worn stones.

On another day, I went by train to see Luxor. I travelled by myself as my cousin had not taken any leave and his wife seemed to be a retiring lady with no interest in antiquities, or maybe had already been there. It was an experience I would have liked to share, but as I had not travelled to Egypt to sit in Cairo sipping tea, I went alone. At these places of interest, there was usually a guide to show one around. Again travelling alone, I went by train to see the Valley of the Kings. The train was primitive by British standards, with wooden seats, but not crowded and quite a few people spoke English and were pleasant and polite. It took quite a while to walk around the various ruins in the Valley of the Kings which was completely different to anything I had seen before and I am glad I had the opportunity to visit there.

Cousin Archie had a flat in Heliopolis, a suburb of Cairo. Discovering at least one mutual interest, his wife took me shopping. I did not buy anything, but enjoyed looking around the main shopping areas. I saw a lot in ten days and enjoyed my holiday but even so, I was quite pleased to get back on board ship to return to cooler climes and to start farming.

On my return home, the local council asked my help to start classes in cheese making. I in turn approached several friends and eventually there were in total eight to ten young girls, including me, making Cheshire cheese under instruction from an expert. This lasted for about six months. Exactly what the benefit was envisaged in running these classes is lost in time. Whether any of the participants continued making cheese, or even what happened to the cheese we made while there, I never knew. We were however judged on our cheeses and I was awarded the highest mark, which was possibly due to my help in getting the classes together and the fact that they were being held in a property belonging to the Lloyd family!

While in her twenties, Iris joined the Voluntary Aid Detachment group, always referred to simply as V.A.D., which had been started by our local doctor's wife. She learnt first aid and used to go to help at the local hospital. Once, after she had been working in the maternity wing, she said to me that being sent there quite put one off having children of one's own. Fortunately, it did not put her off and later she had three children, a boy followed by two girls.

CHAPTER SEVEN

The arrival of Fuchsia and Jonquil

After completing her domestic science course, Iris was keen to go out and get her first job, but my mother was reluctant to loosen the apron strings and persuaded her to stay at home for a while. In frustration, and in an effort to keep occupied, Iris started keeping a few pigs and was taking them to market. At market one day, she met a young mining engineer, Cecil Clarke, who was staying with the Wynne-Eytons, good friends and neighbours of ours in Mold. Their daughter, Violet, was my best friend even though she was twelve years older. Iris and I were bridesmaids at her wedding. Cecil took a great fancy to Iris and started calling around. He was eighteen years older than Iris and anxious to become a married man. Iris was a little unsure, but agreed to marry him. They were married in Mold church on 7 June 1932. Uncle Arthur gave her away and I was one of her bridesmaids. She was a lovely bride all in white and surrounded by her bridesmaids in full-length, forget-me-not blue dresses, a spray of flowers in their hair and carrying small posies. There were six adult bridesmaids and two little ones. One of the little girls was Mary Alice, Aunt Elfrida's granddaughter, the other little girl, Elizabeth Ann, came from my mother's side of the family. The little ones were very young, both less than six-years-old and behaved impeccably. The reception was, of course, at Pentrehobyn and the sun shone on the happy couple.

After spending their first night together in the Berkeley Hotel in London, they went on to Canada for their honeymoon as Cecil had a brother there. When they came back, they bought a lovely property in Cornwall, quite near Falmouth. They settled there and raised a family. Cecil, being a mining engineer, travelled abroad a lot. When one contract involved a lengthy stay in West Africa, Iris went with him. Their young son, Edward (Teddy), was sent to Pentrehobyn with his nanny while they were away. My mother was delighted to have this grandchild in her care. She was very fond of children and often had her brother's four children, Terence, Naomi, Lucien and Gervase to stay. She was particularly fond of Lucien. The children too loved being at Pentrehobyn. Once Iris was married and living in Cornwall, I did not see much of her as our lives followed very different paths. Neither of us were great correspondents. It was not until years later when, as a widow, she came back to live at Pentrehobyn, that we were seen together again.

Then I too fell in love – with a Dexter cow!

A friend and neighbour of mine, Joyce, who, although married, was living with her parents nearby, invited me to come and see the Dexter cows she was raising. This was the first time I had seen this particular breed and I immediately thought 'This is the one for me'. Being such small animals they looked as if they would be easy for a woman to manage. I learned too that they were good for milking as well as beef, so I would be able to make cheese.

Having discovered that a cousin, Lady Kathleen Hare, bred Dexters at Brockenhurst in Hampshire, on the edge of the New Forest, I bought two heifers from her. They arrived in a cattle truck one afternoon and went by the rather grand names of Brockenhurst Fuchsia and Brockenhurst Jonquil. The gardener and I got them unloaded and took them to a pasture where there was a barn ready for them. Dexters are short in stature, either all black or red in colour, and sturdy, gentle animals. They settled in well and I quickly made friends with the two newcomers.

Gradually, I built up a small herd, buying cows from various local people. I sold milk and made butter for the house, and once a week made cream cheese that was sold to a fishmonger in Mold. Each little cheese was wrapped in linen cloth and silver paper and labelled 'Pentrehobyn Dairy'. Making cream cheese used a lot of milk and really I should have had a larger herd to make it profitable, but my cheeses were good and the fishmonger had no problem in selling them.

The Dairy Show was due to start in London. The show had everything pertaining to dairy farming – cows, milk, butters and cheeses on display from all over the country. The show was normally on for three or four days and during that time, judges would be busy assessing the merits of the various animals and the dairy produce put before them. I decided to send in an entry and take one of my cream cheeses to be judged. On arrival in London, I duly went straight to the Dairy Show with my cheese and was horrified to find there were at least twenty cheeses entered in that particular class. I did not think that my humble

Dexters at Pentrehobyn

little cheese stood a chance. My mother had come to London with me and we stayed at the Sesame Club opposite Claridges. She welcomed the chance to visit friends and relatives and do a little shopping. She was not particularly interested in the Dairy Show so I went back two days later on my own – and was both amazed and delighted to find my cream cheese had been awarded third prize.

I joined the Dexter Society and started taking my cows to agricultural shows with not much success to begin with, but it did mean I got to know other enthusiastic breeders. In 1936, I was made President of the Dexter Society, holding office for a year.

While still living at Pentrehobyn, I was asked to help with the Scouts, to be precise the Wolf Cubs. I was called Akela. Akela was the female wolf in *The Jungle Book* by Rudyard Kipling and was the usual name for the leader of the pack in the Wolf Cubs. At the start of each meeting, the cubs would gather round me and chant, 'Akela! Akela! We will do our best'. I organised games and took them camping every year down by the River Alun near Pentrehobyn. There was a competition coming up for the County Shield that caught my eye. As I had a Wolf Cub pack going, I suggested to the boys, aged seven to eleven, that it would be nice to enter. We decided they should go as animals from the *Jungle Book*. I managed to buy some masks of various animals and the boys' parents helped to make the rest of the costumes. The boys thought it was great fun and with the masks on would vie with each other to produce the most frightening sound effects. Growls and roars echoed round the hall. The competition took place at Prestatyn. When it came to the judging, we won first prize and received the much-prized County Shield. The boys and their parents were delighted with that and of course, I was too. I worked with the cubs until the war came and I joined the Wrens. Although I had fun with the cubs, I was not sorry to be giving it up. It was rather time consuming, and I often begrudged the time spent away from my livestock.

As soon as it became obvious that war was imminent, my mother decided to leave Pentrehobyn and to let the house. My sister was by then happily married and living in Cornwall and I was considering joining the Wrens. The house was really too big for just one person. We discussed the problem of the cows and as we were to retain the use of the land, other than the garden close to the house, Mr Sowman, a good man working with me at the time, agreed to look after them. My mother duly went to stay with my sister in Cornwall and I went to London to join up. The house was let through an agent and we had a succession of tenants at Pentrehobyn for many years. One couple, Mr and Mrs Chapple-Gill lived there for twelve years and we became firm friends.

During the war, I would visit Pentrehobyn whenever I could to check on my Dexters as I regarded them an investment in my future. Cecil, my brother-in-law, although in his late fifties, was called up into the Royal Air Force – presumably, they had need of his engineering knowledge and experience. He was in charge of an aerodrome in Gloucestershire and the family let the house in Cornwall and moved to Shrivenham. This was unfortunate as much later I was drafted to Falmouth so would have been very close by and able to visit them. Instead when we did meet up, it was usually in London.

CHAPTER EIGHT

The Wren at war

After war was declared and the immediate feeling of nervous anticipation began to ease, a strong wave of patriotism swept through the land and many people, even those not eligible for active service, began to volunteer to help the war effort in many different ways. As my father had been in the Royal Navy, my thoughts naturally turned to the Women's Royal Naval Service, the Wrens, as they were known. The WRNS was created in November 1917 during the First World War, with the main object to, as their promotional material later urged, 'Free a man for sea service'. Doing precisely that, the WRNS took over many of the on-shore tasks. Cooking, cleaning and serving meals were the immediate jobs filled. In 1919, a year after the war ended, the WRNS was disbanded, but as soon as the Second World War started, there was no hesitation in reforming the service. By 1944, the service numbered 74,000 women, undertaking as many as 200 different jobs, all still on-shore. The WRNS finally disbanded as a separate service in 1993. Women now join the Royal Navy, and the variety of jobs they undertake has been greatly expanded.

Having applied to join the Wrens, I was asked to go for a medical in Chester. Passing that hurdle, a few weeks later I received my call up papers and went to South Kensington for training. This was nice for me as my aunt, Mary Iremonger, was living nearby and I could go and have tea with her occasionally. When I applied to join the Wrens, I told them of my farming interests and asked that I would not be sent overseas.

They made no promises, but I stayed in England for the duration of the war. This was a great relief as, all the time I was serving in the Wrens, Mr Sowman wrote regularly to keep me informed of what was happening back on the farm and, whenever I could take a day or two from my leave, I was on a train back to Pentrehobyn and my precious cows.

I was in my mid-thirties when I joined the Wrens and older than most of the recruits. This often meant taking orders from officers younger than I was, but I never found it to be a problem. I respected their station and the skills they had acquired. I had only been in the Wrens for a week when my uncle, Arthur Lloyd, died. I asked permission to attend the funeral and compassionate leave was granted. My mother and I, together with a cousin, travelled up to Pontblyddyn to stay with friends and attend his funeral. My sister was expecting her third child so could not attend, as the journey up from Cornwall would have been too difficult for her. Both of us were particularly fond of Uncle Arthur so it was sad she could not join us in saying farewell. He is buried in the family plot at Pontblyddyn where my father, and later my mother, were also laid to rest.

The Wrens decided I should become a cook and while at South Kensington, I was sent to train in the galley for about three weeks. Naval terminology was used even on dry land, so the kitchen was always called the galley, though there was not the same space limitation as would be found in a real galley on board ship. It went further; the lounges were wardrooms, the corridors were gangways and even the on-shore facilities were given the names of ships. HMS *Ganges* never sailed out of Shotley!

After acquiring some basic cooking skills, I was sent to HMS *Ganges* in Shotley, near Ipswich. The accommodation there was very nice. Villa-type houses were each shared by eight Wrens. The galley work, however, was a bit daunting. The very first day I was faced with a mountain of potatoes and told to take the eyes out. Thankfully, they had already been peeled mechanically by having been put into a special drum designed for that purpose. On the next day, another mountain of potatoes faced me, and again the day after that. I began to wonder if removing eyes from potatoes was to be the sum total of my war effort.

The main galley, a large kitchen, was quite a rough place and as we were feeding so many men, the work was hard. Every day we prepared and served breakfast, dinner (the main meal of the day) and supper. One was not on duty all day, just long enough to cover a period of two meals before the next shift took over. The canteen was open all day and all night, and food was available at any time. We were catering for more than 200 hungry young men daily, most of them were coming off the ships as they docked. To begin with, I was only involved in cleaning potatoes, other Wrens were preparing other vegetables. Wrens were also busy cooking and serving the food, clearing the tables and washing up. I soon became pretty nifty at 'blinding' potatoes and took my turn at doing a variety of other jobs in the galley. Meals were prepared in advance and kept warm on plates in heated storage compartments ready to be served quickly at any time. In the forces, there was neither rationing nor a shortage of fresh food. We had fresh eggs while the family at home battled to make dried eggs tasty and counted the points remaining on their ration cards.

While at Shotley as new recruits, we also did our fair share of square bashing and learnt all the necessary display skills; whom to salute and when, how to keep our rooms and kit tidy for inspection by the First Officer and so on.

One day, about a month after I started in the main galley, I was told that I was to be promoted to Leading Wren. The ceremony took place on the quarterdeck, not on a ship, but in a designated area within the barracks. Afterwards, the captain told me I was now Leading Wren, I saluted and was given an anchor insignia to attach to my arm. In the

Royal Navy, it is known as a 'hook.' Months, then a year, passed and more and more potatoes were cleaned. It is a wonder I can still look them in the eye, if you will excuse the pun.

Then one day I was called to the Officers Board. I had a bout of 'flu' just before I was due to go and remember feeling very anxious that I might miss the opportunity for promotion if I did not attend. Fortunately, I recovered in time, and waited with about six or seven others to be interviewed. I believe some influence had been brought to bear by a friend of my late father who felt I had been in the galley long enough. The interview was formal and intimidating. Four very senior Wren officers asked us questions. One of these officers I recognised as Lady Cholmondeley who lived about ten miles from my home. We had never actually met, though she would have seen by my home address that I was from Mold. Maybe this helped and I was asked to choose between doing administrative work or 'Quarters' if promoted. They encouraged me to choose Admin, but as I was not very interested in or familiar with office procedure or paperwork, I opted rather for quarters and was pleased that when I got my promotion, my request had been granted. Quarters involved looking after the living quarters of the officers and arranging the catering for them.

Firstly, I was sent to Bristol to Mrs Bell, a first officer who was sister to the Director of the WRNS. I remember that the Director, Vera Laughton Matthews, was nicknamed the 'Giant Panda' but never knew why. Formally, she was addressed as 'Ma'am'. Working under Mrs Bell, I found that it was a bit like running a hotel and I enjoyed doing it. I had been in Bristol for about six months when I was given the choice of staying on there or moving to a port. I opted for the latter though, in hindsight, might have been promoted faster had I stayed in Bristol. Having made my choice, I was sent on to HMS *Beaver* at Grimsby.

It was at Grimsby that I first had what is now recognised as a personality clash with a more senior officer. I suppose in some ways it was inevitable that living and working as closely as we did, problems should arise. I never really knew if the aggressive attitude of this particular acting first officer was directed at me as a person or rather simply because she could not see why there was any need for a quarters officer. She made her views clear and proceeded to make life extremely unpleasant. It reached a point where she could not even bring herself to speak to me. Eventually, I could not bear it any longer and asked to see her. She said she was very busy and would let me know later. Nothing happened for several weeks and so I approached her again. This time I think she felt that she had to see me and I was able to make the formal request for a transfer. She asked my reason and I told her straight that as we did not seem to get along, it would be better if someone else took my place. The stand I had taken was approved of by three colleagues who decided to celebrate my moment of bravado by taking me down to the docks where one could go on board a ship for a few drinks. In wartime, the future was so uncertain and death ever-present, that people, particularly those actively engaged in the forces, tended to snatch every opportunity to relax with a drink. Gin and tonic was the Royal Navy's drink and supplies used to arrive by trawler. There was a bar on the trawler and that is where we went. Everyone smoked in those days too. The four of us made quite a night of it, happily knocking back the gin and tonics and puffing away. Cigarette smoke in a confined space as well as a large amount of alcohol contributed to a pounding head the following day.

I was not feeling too bright that morning when my 'enemy' decided that perhaps she had better make a bit of an effort to work with me and asked to be shown round the quarters. Fortunately, there was nothing wrong and the inspection went pleasantly enough. Both of us knew however, that it was too late for a reconciliation and I made no effort to stop the request for transfer, little dreaming it would cause a furore. Before we knew it, a very senior officer arrived and started to interview us. I told my story as factually and bluntly as I could, and was fortunate

Third Officer Lloyd being presented to HRH the Duchess of Kent, Commandant of the Wrens at HMS Ganges

in that three other junior officers backed me up. In the end, and to my surprise, I stayed and she went! I had stood up for myself and won and this made me feel good. I later heard that this troublesome Acting First Officer was transferred to Dover but soon left the service to start a family. I got on fine with her replacement but she suddenly went AWOL to join her husband, also in the Royal Navy, who had been transferred up north. For a while, I was on my own and then a first officer called Elizabeth Wilberforce arrived and at last things ran smoothly.

At Grimsby, I was promoted to second officer; that meant more pay and more responsibility, and I was then drafted to HMS *Watchful* at Great Yarmouth. There I looked after the Wrens' quarters as well as the Wren Officers' quarters. The quarters for both were in a large, old hotel facing the sea. The officers each had a room to themselves, but the junior ranks had to share. One of my duties was to check that everyone was safely in quarters at night and that was not as easy as it sounds when other duties kept one occupied. I needed help and was lucky to become friendly with Joan Walters who was working as a censor clerk, checking the mail in and out of the barracks. She offered to help me check people in late at night and I was very pleased to accept her help.

One nice thing about Great Yarmouth was that there was a cottage a little inland, for the use of any off-duty Wren officer. One had to cycle to reach it, but the cottage was fully furnished and one could stay the night there if not on duty the following day. It was a chance to forget the war if only for a day. However, even this was not sufficient to ward off the strain of wartime living. Being a port, it was inevitable that Great Yarmouth was targeted for attack. The bombing was bad and I was up nearly every night. The Germans usually waited until dark before attacking and the first we would know of it was when the air raid sirens started wailing. We would immediately head for the shelters and I would try to make sure all those from the quarters were present. One shelter could hold about twenty people; we drank tea and tried to ignore the sounds of war. Outside, the searchlights would be piercing the sky to highlight the enemy and the guns would be pounding, trying to deflect the aircraft from their target, but still the bombs hit the ground with deafening explosions. At last the 'All Clear' would sound and we would emerge and go about our duties as best we could knowing the sirens could go off again at any time. I stayed in my uniform, not changing for bed for weeks on end. Inevitably there came a night when one of our buildings was hit. Eight Wrens were killed that night, including Third Officer Jago Brown, who had been a personal friend. The building had taken a direct hit leaving little that was recognisable. I had to attend the funerals; it was the first time that death had come so close and it affected me deeply. Lack of sleep and stress also began to take their toll and on parade one day, I fainted from exhaustion. I was transferred to what was considered a quieter place, HMS *Forte* at

Falmouth. No sooner had I arrived, than German planes flew over and the Wrens quarters there were bombed but fortunately no one was hurt. Because of the bombing, and the resulting shortage of accommodation, I had to share quarters with a first officer. When she produced a bottle of gin, I knew we would be friends.

At Falmouth, we had carpentry lessons and to this day, I have a small, very heavy, little stool that I made there. I was still in charge of quarters and very happy at Falmouth. Quarters consisted of several houses, each accommodating about twenty Wrens with a separate house for the officers. All these houses had been commandeered for the duration of the war. There was a petty officer in charge at each house to organise breakfast and a light meal in the evening. A canteen provided the main midday meal. The officers had their own cook. I would discuss supplies with her and order them. I had the use of a bicycle to go round from one house to the other and occasionally I would be invited to stay for a meal. I lived in a double-storey house right on the sea front that I shared with my first officer and a few other Wrens. Of course, we still had bombing raids to contend with but gradually they became less frequent.

Then, one day, we realised that the war was at last coming to an end and we could all think of returning home. I was sent to HMS *Drake* at Plymouth until my demob came up. Although asked to consider staying on in the Wrens in peacetime, I declined. I was keen to get back to farming and to find a house big enough so that my mother could come and stay when she wished. It was very sad to leave the Wrens after five-and-a-half years. I kept my uniform, not that it was of much use to me in civilian life, and I kept in touch with the friends I had made. Elizabeth Wilberforce in Felixstowe was one of these. Having eventually lost touch with her, I made some enquiries through a local club there and received confirmation a year ago that she had passed away. Sheila Lightbody is yet another with whom I exchanged visits and reminiscences until both of us were unable to travel. Sheila lived in St Mawes and, like me, received a telegram from the Queen when she reached one hundred. Like me, she also never married. Her good friends telephoned to tell me that she died recently and I grieve.

Interruption ...

The war years were difficult, dangerous and life changing. Although afterwards the pieces were picked up and normality was resumed, people were changed. How could you not be changed when from running a small farming project and dairy, you peeled potatoes? From being your own boss, you had to obey without question. To begin with it was probably exciting, but bombs are not exciting. When Miss Lloyd was telling me about her time in the Wrens it was a while before she mentioned bombs. 'Did you get bombed?' I asked. Silly question as they were at a wartime base for ships and men, a prime target for the enemy. Then she did tell me more but never really expressed the horror and fear that the attacks must have caused. Emotion is not shown. She would not have made good television for people who like to see emotion displayed. Her vocabulary does not include words such as fear, stress or grief. The small joys of life were appreciated more then, shining that much brighter against darkness and sorrow. I believe her when she says she enjoyed her time in the Wrens. Most people who experienced the war felt proud to have helped and proud to have survived and friends made when times are hard are friends for life. The uniform still hangs in a cupboard upstairs.

CHAPTER NINE

Bulls at Ball Hill Farm

The Wrens offered me a job in civilian life, running a sort of boarding house for Admiralty personnel in Bristol. I did this for a while until my friend from the Wrens, Joan Walters, contacted me. She was working at the BBC near Reading as a secretary and told me there was a temporary job on offer there for a cook. I jumped at it and worked at the BBC while I looked for a farm in the south of England. I decided to live in southern England rather than returning to North Wales as the big agricultural shows are in that area. Before the war, I had just the once taken my cattle to a show. I have a strong competitive streak and had such fun that day that I wanted to repeat the experience. Rearing animals is time consuming and socially inhibiting. An agricultural show enables one to meet with others with similar passions, to compete and enjoy a laugh and a drink together afterwards. If successful in the show ring, your reputation as a breeder improves and that is an advantage when you sell your beasts.

The estate agent phoned and said they had a couple of farms that might interest me. Another friend, also working at the BBC, came looking with me just for the fun of it. The first farm we saw was not at all suitable but the second farm, near Newbury in Ball Hill on the Berkshire Hampshire border, was just what I wanted. The double-storey house had three bedrooms. All the rooms were a good size, light, and airy. Everything was in immaculate condition and even more important, there were well constructed outbuildings for the animals. The land

The front entrance to the house, Ball Hill Farm, sketched by Joan Walters

available was just less than 200 acres. Quite a lot of people had been showing an interest in the property but I was lucky in that the woman selling it liked me and said to the agent, 'I would like this lady to have it'.

If I had any doubts, then that comment decided me, and after all the formalities of a surveyor's report, the sale was finalised. I gave up being a cook, became a farmer again, and the very proud owner of Ball Hill Farm.

Furniture that had been left to me by Uncle Arthur came up by van from Mold where it had been stored in the attic at Pentrehobyn, and the next most important task was to get my animals. Four cows came up with Mr Sowman, who had looked after them for so many years during the war. I found accommodation for him nearby. Mr Sowman worked at Ball Hill Farm for five years before he became homesick for Wales and left to return to Flintshire. I then employed a young Irish lad. Once the move was complete, my mother came to stay. We got on very well together. I was busy getting the farm organised, mother was busy in the kitchen and overseeing the garden. It was lovely and great help having her there with me. Both of us wanted to be able to pick vegetables from the garden for use in the house so grew them but we planted some flowers too. In autumn, when it started to feel a bit colder, mother packed her suitcase and went to stay with Iris and her family in Cornwall thus dividing her time equally with her twins.

The arrival of 'Bagendon Teapot' was quite a milestone in my life. Bagendon Teapot from Gloucestershire was my first bull. He was about a year old when I bought him and very beautiful. He settled in quickly and before long, there were calves on the farm. Gradually, the herd built up until eventually I had about thirty cows.

Joan Walters had left her job at the BBC and had gone as a companion to a friend of hers near Reading. It was not working out very well so I suggested she might like to join me and come farming instead. And she did! The two of us lived at Ball Hill Farm for the next twenty-one years. Joan was two years younger than I, knew nothing about farming, but was keen to learn and I was very pleased to have some help with milking the cows and with selling the milk. I planted kale for cattle fodder and found a local farmer willing to bring his tractor and mower to cut grass for me and to bale it. We stored it in the barn for winter feed.

This was an average day on the farm: up at six o'clock with time for a quick cup of tea then off to milk the cows by hand. By eight o'clock, the milk was in the churn and ready for collection at the side of the road outside the farm. Then we had to wash down and clean out the cowshed. That finished, it was back to the house to do the household chores and prepare lunch. I was the cook and Joan the housemaid!

After lunch, I would take the bull out for exercise. With a bull staff hooked into the ring in his nose, I usually had no trouble walking the bull around even though I was of slight build. Dexters, as I said before, are small animals; a Dexter bull although small, is very powerful but fortunately not usually aggressive. I did have trouble with one bull that was only with me for a short time. Bred by Lord Lawther at Penryn, he

With a Dexter bull

went by the rather grand name of 'Lawther Torchbearer'. The bull was tethered in a field and when I went to move him to new grass he strongly objected and decided a game of football would be more fun using me as the ball. He tossed me around somewhat and I could not get back on my feet. The young Irish lad, Michael, was standing in a daze watching and I yelled to him to grab the chain and pull the bull away from me. He eventually managed to do this and I escaped unhurt, other than a few cuts and bruises. Doubting my ability to handle him, Lawther Torchbearer was soon sold.

I had a sheep dog; a black and white border collie called Fly. Although I did not use him as a working dog, he knew what he was and when I took him to a show once, he embarrassed me by herding someone else's sheep. He was a lovely dog and, apart from that one transgression, so easy to handle that I could take him anywhere. The only other livestock on the farm, other than the cattle of course, were a couple of bantams and a cat called Solomon. My little goddaughter, only about four-years-old at the time when she visited the farm, wanted to know the names of all the animals. When I told her the name of the cat, she thought about it for a while and then asked, 'Is he very solemn?' I just laughed.

As a farmer, I learnt to turn my hand to many things. Feeling a chicken-wire fence near the house looked a bit untidy; I decided to replace it with a wall, using concrete blocks. Rome was not built in a day and as there was no particular urgency, the wall was built little by little. It probably was not a prize-winning construction, but it did not fall down while I lived there and is perhaps still standing even now.

I really enjoyed farming and being outside in all weathers. Everyday, I wore corduroy breeches, gumboots, and a black sou'wester when it rained. I was tough and healthy. I went to bed early and slept well. I hardly ever listened to the radio, or had time to read a book, but I did have a daily newspaper. Joan and I got to know a few local people and occasionally would invite friends to come for lunch, but rarely went out in the evening. We also made some friends by going to the local church, though we did not attend regularly. When a new vicar came to the church, Joan was surprised to find it was someone she had met before and was pleased to welcome him.

Iris meanwhile was living a very different life in her home in Cornwall. Only five miles from Falmouth, near a village called Mawnan Smith, Trerose was a large property with a six-bedroomed house set in a beautiful garden and fields that ran down to the Helford River. The children were growing fast and already starting to leave the nest. Teddy had started at Eton, and the two girls, Mary and Susan, were being educated at home, prior to going to Downe House School near Newbury. As it was difficult for me to leave the farm, Iris more often came up to visit me than the other way round. Later, when the girls were at boarding school nearby, I would fetch them for the odd weekend when they were allowed out and when I could fit it in with my increasingly busy schedule. Neither of them enjoyed boarding school but managed to scrape through the necessary examinations. Mary went on to do a domestic science course, and Susan a secretarial course, before they met their future husbands. Both girls were presented at Court, and like us, had to practise their curtsies.

Meanwhile, my little herd of Dexters was thriving. I started showing them and found the excitement of competition, along with the fun of meeting other enthusiasts, very much to my liking.

CHAPTER TEN

Bagendon Teapot and son

Show time, and I took my Dexters to the Royal Show, the Royal Bath and West Show and the Three Counties Show. In the past, the venues of the various shows would change, but now one showground is chosen. As always, it was the cost factor that made the change; now a farmer travels to a show rather than waiting until a show travels near to him. It has also enabled the show societies to build permanent structures to accommodate people and animals. I loved going to these shows and entering either one of my animals or one of my cheeses. Suppliers and manufacturers of various animal foodstuffs looked after their customers at these shows and one would get free lunches and free drinks. The added bonus was the chance to chat with my farming friends.

I learnt a lot from the first show I went to as the animal I took along with wild dreams of walking home with a champion, did not even merit a mention. There was much to learn about how to recognise the best points of a Dexter, in particular how the animal should look when standing before a judge. Quite obviously, the ability of a cow to be milked is one of the points the judges will mark and so will pull on one teat to check that all is well in that department. Dexter cows are dual purpose being both good for milk and beef. My interest was in the dairy. Unwanted bull calves were taken to market to be sold, but if I needed to sell a cow, I would do it privately as good pedigree cows were of value as breeding animals. Obviously, in twenty-odd years of farming there were many occasions when a cow became no longer good for milking and had to be sold for slaughter. Sentiment has no place in farming. Separating cows and calves was another task I dreaded as both would cry out so piteously, but it was necessary to get milk.

Bagendon Teapot and the cow Brockenhurst Jonquil presented me with some very fine calves. Bagendon Teapot himself I did not consider a show animal as he had a kink in his tail that had given him the name of Teapot. Surprisingly, he did win prizes when I entered him in a few shows. Fortunately, his offspring did not inherit this kink and I started taking them to shows.

Taking a cow to a show, or any animal for that matter, involves a lot of preparation. The entry form stating the animal's name and class to be entered into would have been sent in three or four months before the show. Two days before the show we would take the animals by truck to the show grounds where there were sheds partitioned off for livestock. A spare stall next to those allocated for our Dexters was where Joan and I would put our camp beds for the night and set up our little cooking-stove for a cup of tea. I also used to take a tarpaulin to stretch across the entrance to give us some privacy. Not the greatest hotel room, but it was fun. The day before the show was spent grooming the animals; washing, brushing, and trimming. On show day when the steward came to tell us to go to the judging ring, I would put on my white coat and proudly lead the animal out. The judges would be looking at the head, body shape and legs of the

Me with one of my prize winning Dexter cows

animal and frequently came to feel the skin. By the time you were asked to parade around, they had probably already decided who was to receive the rosettes.

It was at the Royal Show in Newcastle-upon-Tyne that I first showed the bull Pentre Hobyn Javelin, bred from Bagendon Teapot. I drove up in my Land Rover with two animals loaded into a trailer, Javelin and a cow called Pentre Hobyn Cherry Ripe. It was a long and tiring trip but well worth the effort as Cherry Ripe was judged Champion Cow and Javelin, Champion of the Yearling Bull Class. On this occasion, my mother came with me and this made me even more delighted at my success.

The following year, I again took Pentre Hobyn Javelin to the Royal Show. Not only did he win his class, but this time he was also named the Champion of the Dexter classes. It was a great thrill and Joan and I went to the Farmers' Club tent to celebrate. I was still wearing my white coat when we went in and was immediately stopped by the secretary who objected to my mode of dress. When I explained the win I was celebrating, he relented, the white coat ignored and the party started. Two years later, I entered Pentre Hobyn Javelin again, with the same satisfying result. The Royal Agricultural Society's Royal Show now has a permanent home in Stoneleigh Park in Warwickshire. I can remember the long journey to Newcastle the first time I showed Javelin but I have shown him too at Stoneleigh Park.

After showing an animal, there was time to enjoy looking around the various commercial stands, most of them closely allied to farming; suppliers and manufacturers of animal feeds and farming equipment for example. Many would offer a free lunch to regular customers so, needless to say, we would be looking for known suppliers at about noon!

When Joan and I were away at shows, I had to have someone looking after the cattle on the farm. A nice man called Mr Reader, who came from Essex, used to come regularly. He was a middle-aged man, possibly retired, with a wife and two young sons. I know little of his background, but he looked after my farm very well and kept in touch long after I left farming, often mentioning in his letters the happy times he spent at Ball Hill Farm.

With the successes I was having with my cattle, I became respected as an expert on the breed and was persuaded to judge. It was Lady Loder who put my name forward to the Dexter Society. She herself had a very celebrated herd of Dexters on her estate near Horsham. Her registered herd name was 'Grinstead'. Lady Loder's knowledge of the breed was extensive and she had been a judge for several years. On her death, her herd was sold. Her son, Sir Giles Loder, was a gardener not a farmer, and became known for the establishment of the wonderful azalea and rhododendron garden called Leonardslea, open to the public and well worth a visit. Having been accepted as a judge, I was asked to judge at all the big shows, including the Royal Agricultural Show, and then one day I was delighted to be asked to judge at the Rand Easter Show in Johannesburg, South Africa. The Dexters bred in South Africa compared very favourably with those in the United Kingdom. Disconcertingly, half way through the judging, a table was brought in with refreshments and all judging stopped while we enjoyed the tea and sandwiches. The competitors were a bit annoyed.

This was my first visit to Africa. Fortunately, my sister Iris and her husband Cecil were also in South Africa at the same time, and in Cape Town on holiday. After my judging duties were over, I flew from Johannesburg to Cape Town and spent some time sightseeing with them. We went up Table Mountain and travelled along the Garden Route. The scenery was spectacular and we had a lovely two-week break before sailing home.

While I was away, Joan was left in charge of the farm. Although she knew nothing about farming or cattle when she first came to live with me, she learned quickly and I was confident that everything would go smoothly in my absence. The little Dexter herd grew, and when there were about ten to fifteen cows to be milked daily, we put in a milking machine and that made milking less of a chore. The farm did well from both milk sales and the sale of cattle each year.

After returning from South Africa, I thought it would be a good idea to have a field day on the farm to demonstrate what it is exactly judges look for in Dexters. I approached Captain Sutton, a well-known judge, and he agreed to come to my farm and give a demonstration. I invited members of the Dexter Society to a stand-up lunch and about twenty people accepted. After the lunch, I paraded several of my animals, and Captain Sutton pointed out and discussed their good and bad points. We were lucky in that the weather was fine and I think everyone enjoyed themselves, as well as learning something more about Dexters.

I had a very good neighbour in Mr Stephen Hutchings, a very obliging man who would come to our aid if we had a task that two women could not handle. He spent quite a lot of time with us and we were a bit concerned that Mrs Hutchings would not like it, but nothing was ever said. I had an idea that Mrs Hutchings did not enjoy being a farmer's wife. She seemed to have none of the domestic skills usually associated with the job, like making butter, bread or jam.

My mother had a fall while dressing in her bedroom. She was ninety-two. Joan kept a cool head in emergencies; she called for an ambulance and made my mother as comfortable as possible until it arrived. Mother was taken to the hospital at Reading where it was found that she had broken her hip. She never walked again and with great reluctance, we made the necessary arrangements for her to go into a nursing home. She was a very private person and found being among strangers upsetting, but I was unable to give her the all day nursing care she required. When her health deteriorated, my sister and brother-in-law came up from Cornwall but were too late to see her alive.

I shall be ever grateful to my father for giving my sister and me a good talking to about saving money and how to handle finances, when we were ten years old. Today, I cannot remember exactly what he said but it made a lasting impression on both of us. Even though my sister married a wealthy man, he told me that she was as careful with money as if she had married a curate. As for myself, in running a farm I had to account for every penny spent and every penny gained to satisfy the taxman as well as for my own information. There was other paperwork to be done too. Records were kept of each cow and each bull, pedigrees were applied for and kept up-to-date. Proof of pedigree was required before an animal could be entered in the herd book and only those entered in the herd book could be shown. A good pedigree plus any show success would increase their future sale value. I had a little office at the side of the house. No typewriter or adding machine, just paper, pens and pencils and a rubber.

CHAPTER ELEVEN

The suitcase is packed

During my life, I have been fortunate to be able to travel quite extensively. I have already mentioned our trips to France and Italy as children, my first solo adventure out to Egypt and judging in South Africa. The next generation of the family also seem to be world travellers. I have a great nephew in the Sudan, another in New York State, and now that travel has become easier and cheaper everyone seems to be off on holiday abroad.

My sister Iris and her husband Cecil also used to travel quite a lot. As a mining engineer, he visited West Africa on business and Iris went with him. Then her daughter Mary married Simon Harvey who was in the Navy and based in Hong Kong, her other daughter Susan married John Gaisford St Lawrence, and they made their home in County Wicklow in Ireland. Iris and Cecil frequently visited the two families, especially once grandchildren started arriving. When they asked me if I would like to join them on a trip to Hong Kong, I was pleased to accept. We travelled by sea, and Mary and Simon met us at the dockside. They were living in a flat in Stanley, a little way from the centre of Hong Kong, and made us very welcome.

In Stanley, there was a very good market and we had fun wandering around and looking at all the wares on offer. There was everything you could think of – vegetables, fruit, fish, clothing, jewellery, ornaments, cameras and electrical goods. All seemed very cheap compared to similar items back home. I found two decorative teapots that I liked very much and bought them as well as a little bamboo stool. Apart from the market there were of course lots of other shops. I was particularly interested in one of many where clothing was made up quickly and cheaply from material chosen there. I had a jacket and skirt beautifully tailored to fit me.

There was a racecourse nearby in Happy Valley and we went to the races, though I did not bet. I am not particularly interested in racing, but have been to watch the Grand National at Aintree a couple of times. The racing at Happy Valley was flat racing. There were many people there so it was obviously a popular pastime locally.

Mary and Simon had booked all of us on a cruise from Hong Kong to Japan on the P & O liner, *Chitral*. The ship was not too big and there were only a few passengers on board so we were well looked after. We visited Tokyo and several other towns and places. The inland sea of

The twins at Mary and Simon's wedding

Japan was a beautiful sight and we saw the famous Mount Fujiama that has been painted by so many artists. We also saw the terrible devastation caused to both Hiroshima and Nagasaki.

While on board *Chitral*, Mary and Simon celebrated their second wedding anniversary and, to their delight, their young son James found his sea legs and started to walk for the first time. We were away for about a fortnight in all before returning to Hong Kong and then home.

I went to Hong Kong again with Iris after Cecil passed away. This time Joan Walters came with us. Joan was a seasoned traveller, having had a job on P & O liners at one time, but she had never been to Hong Kong. She too enjoyed the market and shopping. It was the first time Joan and I had been away on holiday together, usually one or other of us would take a break for a few weeks and stay with friends or relatives. This time we were both away for about three weeks and that was as long as I was happy to be away from my animals.

My other travelling companion of later years was Madeleine Chapple-Gill. After renting our house near Mold for twelve years, she and her husband moved into their own home near Welshpool. Sadly, their marriage ended in divorce and Madeleine moved to Nant Mawr. When I moved to Llangynog, I was pleased to have someone I knew living so close. As a travelling companion, Madeleine suited me very nicely. However, she tended to be very outspoken and occasionally I found myself having to smooth a few ruffled feathers here and there.

We went on safari to Kenya together and stayed at the very famous Treetops for one night. I loved the sights and sounds of the African bush and it was fascinating to watch the various wild animals coming down to the waterhole to drink. There were elephants, lions, zebras, giraffes and many other smaller creatures. That trip was so successful and enjoyable that Madeleine and I went to Africa again, this time to the Ngorongoro Crater in Tanzania. We saw a lot of game on the Great Plains and I particularly remember the huge herds of zebra that outnumbered even the wildebeest. We also had a close encounter with an elephant that followed the tour car we were in and gave us a few anxious moments before deciding we really were not worth stomping on!

Our final trip together was completely different being a cruise to Norway where we feasted our eyes on the beautiful scenery of the fjords. The ship stopped at various small ports and at each, we went ashore to look round the local shops. The cruise went right up into the Arctic Circle and we saw icebergs and a few whales, but mainly it was the spectacular scenery that was the attraction. Personally, I prefer watching animals to admiring scenery, however spectacular!

When we were in our eighties, my sister Iris and I had one rather special holiday together. She was already a widow, and her health was not as good as mine. We went to Madeira and stayed in the very well known Reid's Palace Hotel. Iris was having difficulty walking so stayed in the hotel for the most part, relaxing and enjoying the warm weather. We shared a lovely room with a magnificent view of the sea and it had a large terrace where we could sit and enjoy the sunshine. The hotel did not serve lunch and, as we were accustomed to eating at midday, I would go out in the morning to buy us both some light snack. The rest of the time we would just talk. Although our lives had followed different paths, we still had that special bond enjoyed by sisters and, in particular, twin sisters. It is nice to look back and remember that time we had together.

While we were on Madeira I was surprised and curious, to notice that there was no sign of any cattle around, although there was always fresh local dairy produce at the hotel. I enquired about this and was told that cattle on Madeira were kept in barns and not allowed to graze freely in the fields. I was horrified at this for it seemed to me as bad as battery chickens, though the argument was that as they had never been out of the barn they did not miss the open air. I did not have the chance to verify this story and hope to this day it was not true.

The last trip I took abroad was to Turkey. I was persuaded to go by my niece Susan and cousin Anne Delves–Broughton. I am not sure why they wanted an old lady of ninety along but I was game to travel with them. We stayed in Istanbul and went by boat to the Princes Islands. I cannot remember very much about the holiday except that I bought two rugs!

But I am getting ahead of myself in time, and my story is not yet told so we will now travel back to the late nineteen-sixties.

I reluctantly decided that the time had come to leave the farm. Various factors influenced this decision to move on. The first being that Joan had to leave me as her mother was unwell and she had to go and look after her. Joan must have found this a difficult period as she and her mother did not get on too well together. Her mother, a widow, had lived alone for many years and obviously was used to doing things a certain way and, as both were strong willed women, fights were inevitable. When her mother died, Joan moved to a cottage in the New Forest near Lymington and I visited her there several times.

My seventieth birthday was coming up and I felt that I was getting too old to continue running the farm on my own. That was the second reason, and the final thing to tip the scales and make the decision easier in a way was that I learned that the house in Llangynog was unoccupied.

CHAPTER TWELVE

My mountain is called Rhiwarth

The house in Llangynog was where my Uncle Arthur had lived for many years and, after his death, had been let to various tenants. I inherited this property from my father. Not just the house, but the Llangynog estate that included several other cottages, a farm and a side of Craig Rhiwarth. My sister, as the eldest twin, had inherited the family home and estate near Mold.

I had visited Uncle Arthur in Llangynog many times and had become known in the village. This made it easier for me when the time came to move into Groes Ffordd. The name means Cross Roads, Uncle Arthur changed it from the original Rock House.

The sale of Ball Hill Farm took quite a long time. I was advised by the estate agents to sell off part of the land separately, as potential buyers were more interested in the house on its own rather than as a farm. It was sad in a way to see it divided like that, but I was moving on and not looking back. Parting with my beloved Dexters was particularly hard; I sold most of them privately. Eventually everything was sorted out, the removal van came for the furniture and I set off for Wales.

Llangynog is on the road from Oswestry to the lake at Bala and the beginning of Snowdonia. The winding road from Oswestry follows the River Tanat and the mountains on either side are beautiful in all seasons. Llangynog is the last village in the Tanat valley before the road climbs over the Berwyn Mountains to drop down to Bala. When I moved to Groes Ffordd, the village had two pubs, a post office that doubled as the village shop, a bank and a general store. There was even a petrol station. Sadly, all except the pubs have now gone and the villagers have to travel three miles to the nearest village shop in Pen-y-bont-fawr, and further still for the services of a bank and for petrol. A post office opens twice a week in the village hall, but is in danger of being one of the services to be withdrawn next.

Groes Ffordd is a slate-roofed house, built of local stone. Very solid, it sits under Craig Rhiwarth looking down the main road through Llangynog. The main road bends to the left less than a hundred yards before the house and starts up the hill to go over the Berwyn Mountains to Bala. The broad access road to the house from the main road divides in front of the house. Turn left, and this small road is the old Bala road that goes up the hill parallel-to, but higher than, the newer main road and then slips back to link again. The residents of the small cottages and bungalows that sit either side use this road. Turn right, and you are on a single-track lane that winds past several farmhouses back to the village

Groes Ffordd, at the foot of Craig Rhiwarth, looking down the road through Llangynog

of Pen-y-bont-fawr. Walkers with boots, windcheater jackets, packs on their backs and woolly hats trudge past, heading a little way up this narrow road before following a bridle path and climbing up through patches of slate strewn track that will eventually bring them to the top of the waterfall, Pistyll Rhaeadr.

Craig Rhiwarth is known locally as Craig-y-Llan, the mountain belonging to the village. Climb up Craig Rhiwarth and you will see the old slate quarry. Climb further to the top and you will come to what is believed to be the remains of a Roman settlement. The land is free for any walker to explore and is a National Heritage site. The two cottages either side of Groes Ffordd are part of the Llangynog estate. Ivy Cottage on the Old Bala Road is the smallest of the three, having only two bedrooms, but it is very charming. Its garden in the summer is a mass of roses and wild flowers lovingly tended by its present tenant, Vera Symonds. A caring friend, Vera regularly visits me and keeps me up to date with village life. The other cottage, Mount Quarry, has three bedrooms and has recently been let to a young family.

Craig Rhiwarth has heather, gorse and bracken growing on it, with small waterfalls running down it, and supplies good grazing for sheep. The sheep come from Glan Hafon Farm that is also part of the Llangynog estate. Glan Hafon is leased to the Evans family who have been there for about twenty years. Ann Evans opens the house to accommodate bed and breakfast guests in the summer season. The village attracts quite a few visitors in the summer months and there are two or three caravan park settlements to accommodate them. Llangynog now has a mixed population. There are Welsh families that have lived here for generations and newcomers who have settled here and one hears Birmingham, London and other accents mingled in with the lilting Welsh. Welsh is spoken frequently and at the junior school in the next village the children are taught in Welsh. I gather that non-Welsh speaking children learn the language quite quickly and have been known to progress by choice to a Welsh-speaking high school.

Uncle Arthur

Groes Ffordd has four bedrooms. At the front of the house, Uncle Arthur had built a conservatory over the original, rather steep steps that led up to the front porch. A new entrance was made to the right and the conservatory, being an extension of the porch, helps to keep the house that much warmer in winter. After I moved in, I had several alterations made. There was an old kitchen range in the left front room. I wanted to use this room as my dining room and the old range had to be taken away. At the back of the house, I added a cloakroom and a toilet. Upstairs, my uncle had a bathroom with a very large bath. This bathroom led off the main bedroom and could only be accessed through that bedroom. This would obviously be inconvenient should other guests be staying so I reduced the size of the bedroom to make an access passage. Once all the alterations were completed, it was painted throughout and I chose to keep it either white or a warmer cream colour to maximise light. Most of my furniture has been inherited and much of it used to belong to Uncle Arthur. Some items he had collected on his travels and I have a very interesting screen that he bought in China. It stands about five-feet high and has two panels framed by bamboo. The intricate embroidery and appliqué worked on a red ground tells a story, though unfortunately for me it will always remain a mystery story. The embroidery is protected by glass. I have another embroidered screen, again glass protected, that stands about four-feet high, and was worked by my grandmother. There is no mystery about this one as it shows a large macaw with two small dogs sitting below its perch.

On the walls I have a few paintings. Two are copies of paintings that hang at Pentrehobyn and which Iris lent to me when I first went to Ball Hill Farm. One of them hangs in the dining room and is a large painting of my great grandfather, Lieutenant-Colonel Iremonger of Wherwell Priory, on horseback with his gamekeeper Watkins standing in front of him. The gamekeeper is quite a portly man, carrying a gun, with a large black and tan dog standing by him. There are two spaniel type dogs nearby obviously ready to retrieve any game. The other copied painting hangs in the drawing room and is of some great, great, great uncle, Joshua Iremonger, who was not as famous as the artist for whom he sat. I wonder if he knew that?

Most of my paintings are of either relatives or cows. The best of the cow paintings is in the drawing room, three cows painted by a Dutch artist. They are not Dexters, but some mixed breed, possibly a short horn cross. The little watercolours upstairs are of my Dexters, painted by a Belgian refugee living near Pentrehobyn and given to me. I have never bought a painting, I have inherited, borrowed or been given them by friends. There is one very striking portrait and the subject is not a Lloyd, but my friend Joan Walters. It was painted by a friend of Joan's sister, and the same sister passed it on to me after Joan died. When I die the painting will go to Joan's nephew.

After changing my new quarters to my liking, I was free to get to know the local people and join in village life. A good start was to become involved in the church. As with all small communities, anyone willing to help with anything was welcomed. Apart from the Anglican church of St Cynog, there were three chapels in the village. The Welsh have always been predominately chapel folk. But times have changed, and even in this peaceful valley, both chapel and church struggle to continue with dwindling congregations. One chapel is now a dwelling house and the remaining two are considering amalgamation. Yes, people still want the village church, but few attend services regularly and those that do have to devise ways of raising money to keep their church going.

Interruption ...

This book has been written in the house at Llangynog, and while writing this chapter with her, I started looking around and realised that all the furniture and some paintings were indeed inherited. Miss Lloyd has never set foot in a furniture store. Never come home clutching swatches of material to get curtains to match the carpet. Perhaps that was the advice her father gave his daughters; never spend money on furniture unless you have to. If the chair was good enough for Uncle Arthur, it's good enough for you, so why not use it? And so the house does not reflect her personality but in spite of that, it is not unwelcoming.

CHAPTER THIRTEEN

St Cynog and the little hare at Pennant Melangell

The church, next to one pub and opposite the other, is dedicated to St Cynog, a Celtic saint, whose name also gives you Llangynog which translated means church of St Cynog. My mother, my sister and I were trustees to my uncle's estate and we arranged for a reredos, a wood panelling encircling the altar, to be put in the church in his memory and onto which is attached a small brass plate.

TO THE GLORY OF GOD
AND IN LOVING MEMORY OF
CAPTAIN
ARTHUR ATHELWOLD IREMONGER LLOYD
D.S.O., O.B.E.
THIS REREDOS WAS ERECTED BY
HIS SISTER-IN-LAW AND NIECES
OF PENTRE HOBYN.
1941

To my knowledge, my uncle could neither speak nor understand Welsh, but he always attended the services at St Cynog even though the local worshippers were all Welsh-speaking and most of the services were taken in Welsh.

I too went regularly to the morning service at St Cynog, but by then English was the chosen language. The vicar, the Reverend Davies, took the service. When he died, his wife stepped into his shoes and the

Pennant Melangell.

Reverend Evelyn Davies looked after the spiritual needs of Llangynog until she was sent to another parish. The Reverend Linda Mary Edwards replaced her. Whoever is vicar of St Cynog also cares for the little church of St Melangell and lives in a cottage nearby. This church is about three miles from Llangynog and is now quite an attraction for tourists who make their way up the narrow road along the valley to visit it. The Reverend Linda Mary spends much time working as a counsellor and has found this particular aspect of her ministry fulfilling, but time consuming, so now has relinquished her duties at St Cynog and the church has a new vicar, the Reverend Edward Yendell who lives near Lake Vyrnwy at Llanwddyn. He has a quartet of churches to look after; ours at Llangynog, plus the churches at Pen-y-bont-fawr, Llanrhaeadr-ym-Mochnant and Llanwddyn. As I am unable to get to church any more, he visits me once a month to allow me to celebrate communion. He comes on a weekday as Sundays must be far too busy.

Reverend Linda Mary still lives in the cottage by Pennant Melangell and looks after the little church and, of course, the counselling centre.

There is a charming story to explain the founding of the little church of St Melangell in such an isolated though beautiful place. Melangell came originally from Ireland, having left to escape from a marriage planned for her. After much wandering, she found a place of peace and refuge in this little valley in the Berwyn Mountains and pursued a life of religious contemplation and prayer. One day, a local prince was hunting in this valley and chasing a hare. The hare took refuge under the skirts of a maiden. The huntsman is surprised when his hounds will not go near her and finds, when he tries to blow his horn, it is as if he were paralysed. The maiden tells the prince her story and says that all she wants is to spend a life of prayer in this valley. The prince is moved by her sincerity, gives her land in the valley, and promises too that hares will always be protected there. Melangell then stayed in the valley where other women seeking the same peace and refuge joined her, and the little church they founded became known as a place of healing. Quite recently, during the years 1988–92, the whole church was restored. During the restoration, the grave of Melangell was discovered and is now incorporated in the chancel.

Inside the church there are several charming carvings of the hare. At the back of the church, is a small souvenir area and stairs that lead to an upper room. On the walls of the stairwell and in the room above, are photographs of the village and its people. There are old black and white photographs of solemn people keeping still for the camera and colour photographs of more recent events. These include a photograph taken at the Millennium of as many residents as were willing to be recorded for posterity. It is a delightful place and is visited by many people; walkers holidaying in the area and others, who like Melangell, come seeking peace and refuge.

The tradition of healing is maintained; the modern pilgrims are cancer patients and their families who come there for counselling and spiritual help. The Prince of Wales' Trust was involved in helping this centre and Prince Charles himself visited in 1996 to see both the centre and the little church. The Reverend Evelyn Davies, who received an MBE for her work with cancer patients, organised a tea party in the vicarage garden in his honour. Because the garden is not large, less than twenty people were invited and all were asked not to tell anyone Prince Charles was to be a guest. I was then walking with the help of a zimmer frame and was seated on a chair in the garden when Prince Charles came over to speak to me. I immediately started to get to my feet but he said, 'Please don't get up'. I told him that I was suffering with arthritis and he sympathised, saying his grandmother had arthritis too.

Before Christmas, there was usually a village fair and soon it was accepted that I would be in charge of the produce stall. I used to buy in many of the vegetables from the weekly market in Oswestry, and other church members kindly donated more vegetables, as well as fruit and preserves. As it was close to Christmas, Father Christmas usually attended and distributed small gifts to the village children.

I also decided to join the British Legion. The nearest meeting place was at Llanfyllin, a small town about nine miles from Llangynog travelling towards Welshpool. The council offices for the area are there and so too is the main medical centre. A second medical centre is a little closer at Llanrhaeadr-ym-Mochnant. The women's section of the British Legion met in a hall in Llanfyllin once a month. Because I had spent five-and-a-half years in the Wrens, I felt that joining the British Legion was the right thing to do. Once a year, on Poppy Day, all the members are involved in selling the poppies to raise money for the aid of ex-servicemen in need. After about five years, when I could no longer drive, I gave up my membership for, although Llanfyllin is so near, there is no direct bus route to it.

Llangynog was a mining village at one time and lead and slate were mined here. My grandfather was involved in slate mining; the slate was split by hand and when this method became too expensive the industry stopped and the village as we knew it slowly began to die. The shops closed, the bank left and the petrol station is now a dwelling place, but the two pubs survived.

Every August, there is a flower show at the Memorial Hall. Not only flowers are exhibited; there are also other competitive sections such cake making, garden produce and handicraft. I always entered in the flower section. Even in my 101st year I got first prize for a maidenhair fern and second prize for an orchid. It is a pleasant village gathering with raffle tickets being sold, and tea and cakes being served. For the past six years, I have always managed to get a first prize for various different entries.

For anything other than basic food items, one has to travel to Oswestry, about eighteen miles away. I had a Vauxhall, one of several I have owned. I learnt to drive when I was about eighteen-years old and to start with drove the family car when at home. After the war, I bought a little car and later, when farming, I bought a Land Rover. I stopped driving in my eighties and it was fortunate then that milk and meat were delivered, and a supermarket in Welshpool also delivered to the house, so a phone call was all that was necessary. I could get a bus into Oswestry should I need to get other items or go to the bank.

CHAPTER FOURTEEN

Old friends depart

My good friend Joan Walters was finding life in the New Forest a bit lonely after her mother died so when I told her Ivy Cottage next door to me was vacant, she sold her cottage and joined me in Llangynog. It was good to be together again but sadly, it was not for long. Joan began to act strangely. She started by accusing the neighbours of taking things from her house and they all became a bit wary of her, but to spare my feelings did not mention anything of that to me and I was unaware that trouble was brewing. Then one day, she begged me to come and stay with her in Ivy Cottage as she was feeling lonely. I eventually agreed and took my night things over to her cottage and we spent a pleasant enough evening together before retiring to bed. In the middle of the night, the bedroom door was flung open and there was Joan demanding to know what I was doing there, and I found myself going home in my night attire. She became more and more unpredictable and odd. Eventually, the doctor advised that she should move into a nursing home in Oswestry. This was arranged and I would visit her there. She always knew me. I looked after her little Pekinese, Sabre, who fortunately got on well with my own little crossbreed, Gemma, who was part miniature Collie and part Corgi. The Pekinese was a rather bad tempered little thing, but he lived the rest of his life with me.

One day Joan went missing and was eventually found wandering around the town. The staff said they thought she was in fact trying to find me. Her nephew, John Walters, then stepped in to help and took full responsibility for her welfare. Her mental state deteriorated further and she was moved to a hospital nearer Shrewsbury. I still visited and she still knew me. Joan was in her late eighties when she died. I went to the service at the crematorium. It was the first and I hope the last cremation service I attend. Her ashes were taken back to Lymington in Hampshire where her parents are buried.

Life in a small village is always busy. I liked to be involved though most of my spare time was spent in my garden. I am definitely an outside rather than an inside person.

Living a life on a farm, caring for animals and going out whatever the weather, I was lucky in that I mainly had very good health. I rarely had a day in bed with either a cold or 'flu'. As children, both my sister and I had all the usual children's illnesses; there were no immunisation programmes as there are today. We had chicken pox, measles, whooping cough, mumps and German measles. Then, in our teenage years, we really hit a low patch. First Iris had rheumatic fever that I believe left her with a weakened heart, and then I went down with diphtheria. Both these illnesses were potentially life-threatening and my poor mother had a very worrying time. After that, we were both pretty strong and healthy and the only time I had bothered doctors was when I broke my arm while still farming in Newbury. I was driving a Land Rover when suddenly the rear prop-shaft broke and the car spun on to its side. A nearby cottager came to my assistance and gave me a cup of tea until medical help arrived. I had my sheepdog, Fly, with me that day and she had to wait, tied-up outside the hospital, while I had my arm plastered and then an ambulance took us both home.

In 1992, my sister Iris had a heart attack and was taken to Wrexham hospital. I was driven over to see her there and after two days she was allowed to go home. Sadly, a few weeks later she had another heart attack and died at Pentrehobyn. The rheumatic fever she had as a child may have weakened her heart but it served her very well for eighty-nine years. The funeral was at Nercwys, about five miles from Pentrehobyn, and she was buried there with her husband. I miss her very much. Her family, Teddy, Mary and Susan all visit me as often as they can manage.

Interruption ...
Miss Lloyd tells me that her grandparents are also buried at Nercwys but her father fell out with the vicar there before he died, hence they decided on Pontblyddyn as a last resting place. Not quite sure why Cecil Clarke, who died in his beloved Cornwall, and who came originally from southern England, decided on Nercwys. Perhaps to be certain that Iris would one day join him, which she did. Maybe he just left it to Iris to decide. Miss Lloyd has her spot booked at Pontblyddyn and that it is just across the road from a pub. She reckons they might serve spirits!

In 1984 I decided it was time to hand over the Llangynog estate to my niece Mary and her husband Simon. More recently, Simon has also been handling all my financial affairs and I am very grateful to him. Iris's eldest child, Teddy is living at Pentrehobyn.

Llangynog celebrated the Millennium by asking all its village folk to gather on a field near the Memorial Hall to have a photograph taken. Afterwards, I was asked to present some Millennium mugs to the children and I made a little speech before they came up to receive them. Other mugs were available for adults to purchase if they wished. Finally, I was asked to plant a tree near the entrance to the hall. The hole had already been dug and everything prepared, so planting the tree was easy.

Breaking another bone unfortunately changed my life. In my early nineties, I fell quite badly, slipping on the path as I was hurrying to get ready to welcome a friend joining me for coffee. Help was quickly on hand and I was carried into the house to await the arrival of the doctor. Two doctors arrived, one was my GP, Dr Hancorn. I do not remember who the other doctor was or why there were two. They were not sure if

I had broken my leg or my hip but in any case, I was taken by ambulance to the Orthopaedic Hospital at Gobowen near Oswestry. X-rays showed it was my hip that was damaged and a hip replacement operation was necessary. After the operation, I was transferred to the Welshpool Hospital to recuperate. The family all rallied round and it was decided that I now needed help in the house. I could still walk with the aid of a zimmer frame, but was very slow. To start with, a woman came every morning from the village to clean the house and I had a chair-lift installed to get me up and down the stairs.

Determined to stay in my own home, I managed like that for quite a while. Had I been forced to move into a nursing home it would have killed me! At that time, I was sleeping in the front bedroom upstairs in a comfortable, but old-fashioned, high bed. When my niece Mary visited, she suggested that perhaps it would be easier if the bed was moved downstairs and so it was. I would still go upstairs to have a bath and a special chair was purchased to lower and raise me in and out of the bath. When I could no longer manage this on my own, Sue Jones, a trained nurse, living in the next village of Pen-y-Bont-fawr, came in every morning to help me. One morning, when getting out of the high bed, now downstairs, I caught my foot in the bedclothes and fell. I lay on the floor wondering how to summon help. It seemed ages that I lay there though it probably was not very long. Suddenly I heard a shout and looked up to see this 'angel' clambering in through the sash window to get to me, the front door being locked. My right arm was broken, so off I went to hospital again. I spent quite a long time in hospital and this caused another problem, in that my old arthritic knees decided I should stop walking and when I returned home, I could not walk any distance even with assistance.

CHAPTER FIFTEEN

My house and Oliver

After my last fall, it was again suggested that I move into a nursing home, a suggestion I again fought against. Social Services then organised a care package that enabled me to stay in my house, Groes Ffordd. To start with, an army of different carers arrived and we coped but it was not entirely satisfactory. People were coming in for short periods, anything up to three different carers in one day and at the weekends, occasionally someone would stay the night. These girls were very kind, and one little Welsh woman in particular became a friend and still visits me. Her name is Llinos.

Eventually, Mary and Simon heard of an agency that supplied carers prepared to live in and we changed to that arrangement. A carer will come and stay for a fortnight or three weeks before there is a changeover and a new carer takes over. Many of the carers are from overseas and so far we have all got on fine. As do most elderly people, I find it difficult to accept strangers into my home, so I prefer to welcome back carers that have been before rather than get to know yet another stranger. Every morning, I am woken at 7.30 by the resident carer and another carer, Margaret, who lives locally. Come rain or shine, Margaret walks up through the village, arriving in time for the morning ritual that has me clean and tidy and in my comfortable chair by 8 o'clock. A quick cup of coffee, a little gossip and Margaret is off to help others start their day.

Occasionally I go out, but it is not easy transferring from the wheelchair into a car so I wait for the world to come to me and through newspapers, television and visiting friends, it does.

I have another companion and it is to him that I am dedicating this book. His name is Oliver. Oliver is a Yorkshire terrier, and rather spoilt but a great companion. He came from Battersea Dogs Home and by the time my niece Mary brought him to me he was very unsettled. He spent the first night shut up in my bedroom and howled his head off. I got no sleep and wondered how I was going to cope. The next night he was quiet but would not eat during the day. I kept calling the vet for advice. A few days later, Oliver decided that he quite liked this new home and he quite liked this new mother.

He sleeps on my bed at night and he sleeps on my bed when I have a rest in the afternoon. When he goes for a walk with the carer, he walks slowly until turned to go home and then it is all systems go; coughing and spluttering as he pulls against the lead in a frantic effort to get back

A happy 100th birthday

to mother and home. I tell him that he is beautiful and that his name is 'Oliver' and occasionally get rewarded by a lick-kiss. He has good hearing and barks to let me know if anyone approaches and he is a gentleman with other dogs. When my niece Mary and husband Simon visit, Oliver plays host to Rosie and Sam, two Norwich terriers. He can get a little jealous though should Rosie demand too much attention from me. In short, we two are a mutual admiration society and I would recommend an Oliver to anyone.

For my 103rd birthday, I was given a kitten. He is completely black and elegantly slim, and has grown from a friendly, skinny kitten into a self-possessed and confident cat and I have named him 'Simon'. Simon was the name of the black and white cat that was awarded the animal equivalent of the VC for his bravery and rat-catching dedication whilst on board HMS *Amethyst*, the ship that came under fire in the Yangtze River in 1949. Oliver was both intrigued and keen to welcome the kitten when he first arrived, but Simon shut his eyes and ignored him and Oliver lost interest. A week later, a toy on a string was dangled in front of Simon and, as any kitten would, Simon started to play. Oliver abruptly sat up and watched and one could see the penny drop, 'My goodness, it's a cat!'

Simon is unafraid of Oliver and will lie in wait and pounce on him. Oliver tries to ignore such indignities, but if Simon gets too boisterous, he will warn him with a short, snarling bark. It is interesting to see that

when either of the animals is taken to the vet the other makes a point of checking all is well upon his return. The friendship is there and I love them both.

Oliver came with me to Pentrehobyn on the 13 October 2003 to celebrate my 100th birthday. The day started with gifts and cards to open. Then, at about 10 o'clock in the morning, a special messenger arrived with the congratulatory message from the Queen. My two nieces, Mary with her husband Simon, up from Suffolk and her younger sister Susan, who had travelled from Ireland, were also staying at Groes Ffordd with me. Vera Symonds, who lives next door in Ivy Cottage and Mary Warne, a long time friend from the village, joined us. We travelled in two cars to Pentrehobyn where my nephew Teddy and his wife Carinthia were waiting for us with a few other friends. We had a very nice lunch party. There was my favourite, roast pork; we drank champagne and at the end of the meal a large cake was brought in. It had many candles on it, but not one hundred. Teddy's grandchildren helped to blow out the candles. We came back to Llangynog fairly soon after lunch to give me the chance of a snooze before more guests arrived in the evening. The house was bursting with people and flowers. It really was quite an amazing day.

Since then, I have had the Queen's telegram framed and it now has pride of place in my drawing room on top of the television. Strangely enough, years ago, a fortuneteller looked at my hand and told me I was going to live a long time.

Other than no longer being able to move around, I am in good health. The eight different pills taken each morning no doubt contribute to my well-being. My sight is not too good, but with the help of a magnifying glass, I am still able to read the newspaper each morning. I enjoy my food, and every evening I enjoy a glass of whisky with ginger ale. I can still write a short note, but this book is being typed on a laptop computer, either to my dictation or after some discussion about remembered events, put down in the writer's own words and then read to me for approval. Many people have asked me to what do I attribute my great age. I don't really have an answer to that, but I have answered a few other questions.

Do you have a favourite colour?

My favourite colour is pink.

In your lifetime there have been many changes, which do you feel had the most significance?

Transport. Both cars and air travel. I enjoy air travel, as I tend to suffer with seasickness when travelling by boat. The other invention that I also appreciate is the telephone. My nieces and nephew do visit me when they can, but they phone quite often so I never feel out of touch.

Were there any advantages or disadvantages in having a twin sister?

Advantages only. We were always close, even when apart and we always enjoyed each other's company when together.

You donate to a lot of animal charities, do you give to any others, cancer research for example?

I support the Dexter Cattle Society and St Dunstans. St Dunstans because serving in the war I knew so many people who were blinded.

What do you consider the worst disability that comes with old age, hearing loss, sight loss, or lack of mobility?

Arthritis.

If you had been born a man what difference do you think it would have made to your life?

I think for a man it is much easier. There are a lot of things a man can do that a woman can't. I might have travelled further!

How would you describe your life?
Some people live a happy life, others a long life. I am blessed because I have had both

If you could go back for a day to any period of your life when would that be?
The day my bull, Pentre Hobyn Javelin, was declared Champion of all Dexters at the Royal Show.